Made in Heaven

D1100483

By the same author:

Letters from the Desert
The God Who Comes
In Search of the Beyond
Love is for Living
Summoned by Love

CARLO CARRETTO

Made in Heaven

translated by
ALAN NEAME

Darton, Longman and Todd

First Published in Great Britain in 1978
by Darton, Longman and Todd Ltd
89 Lillie Road, London SW6 1UD

This translation © 1978 Darton, Longman and Todd Ltd

Originally published in italian
as *Famiglia, piccola chiesa* by Editrice AVE

All biblical quotations are from
The Jerusalem Bible
© 1966 Darton Longman and Todd and Doubleday and Co Inc

ISBN 0 232 51352 X

Printed in Great Britain by
Fletcher & Son Ltd, Norwich

Nihil Obstat R. J. Cuming, D.D., *Censor*
Imprimatur Timothy J. Firth, V.G.
Westminster, 17th February, 1978

Foreword

addressed to the old, but **not** to the young

When this book appeared under the title *Famiglia, piccola chiesa* in 1949, it caused an incredible commotion in Italy. That a priest, let alone the president of the Catholic Action Youth Movement, should have written it, seemed the most shocking of things!

What a closed and air-tight environment we must have been living in, for right-thinking Christians to have taken such offence at such very harmless words of advice. Why, it was even rumoured that the Holy Office would intervene as in olden days over some pernicious heresy! And the second edition had to be held back until the furore had died down.

I can't help smiling over all this now and marvelling at how much the world has changed in the meantime. Most people would agree today, I should think, that it is no bad thing for the young to dream a little and that nothing is more delightful or rewarding than love's young dream. And that the young should idealise each other a little before marriage and so lay the foundations of a lasting mutual respect and a sanctified married life, was all my intention in writing what I did.

In preparing young people for marriage, as also in
writing this book, I have always borne two principles in mind. The *magisterium* of the Church has impressed these on me, and I feel them deeply embed-
ded in my own conscience in any case. They are:
1) Never to go into anatomical details and never to
let myself talk about love as though it were a
physiological mechanism.

It was right to leave the mystery, the veil over
love, that veil and mystery being prefigured in that
symbolic Biblical gesture by which God covered the
nakedness of our first forefathers with clothes which
he himself had made for them. 'Yaweh God made
shirts of skins for Adam and his wife, and clothed
them'. (Gn 3:21).
2) Never to erect an antithesis between the dream of
marriage and the dream of virginity; never to
obscure the issue by hiding from the young the
possibility of the 'great call' to a more sublime and
heroic life of total self-giving to God.

This foreword is addressed to the old and not to
the young; the book, however, was written for the
young and not for the old.

Let us be clear about this. The twenty-year-olds
are the ones who can get something out of it, not
people in their forties. The young have this sort of
poetry in their hearts; the old no longer do.

It is not my business to write about what happens
after marriage: God has willed for me to walk
another road and it would be presumptuous of me to
try and give advice to married people. This book
was written for people who were engaged, and it

sprang from my heart under the promptings of
young Catholics everywhere in the post-war period,
they occupying so great a part of my life and helping
me to clarify the problems of faith and human existence.

I certainly had a dream, and many of the young
dreamed with me.

And I hope that today's young people will go on
dreaming a bit too, as they endure obsessive bom-
bardment by a world in which reading matter,
shows and the streets have transformed love into
eroticism and the mystery of life into a frantic and
no longer soothing coupling of bodies.

It may be that I am mistaken, in which case
please believe that I meant well.

Carlo Carretto

Contents

1. Sadness

Seaside resort. Night. I was walking along, looking for a hotel. Everywhere was full up. On the pavement ahead of me stood a woman, looking at me. Why was she staring? Could she know me?

Why don't I recognise her?

When I pass her, it dawns on me – she gives me a nudge and whispers, 'Want to come home with me, darling? It's only just round the corner.'

I feel unbearably upset. I feel as if my heart has stopped. Were I to look at my reflection in that shop window, I should look as white as a sheet – that I know. But I haven't the time. I don't turn round. I quicken my pace. I very nearly run.

If only the sea were nearer, to wash all the miseries of love away with its bitter waters!

*   *   *

An ugly, soulless village. A knot of people standing outside a house. How pale they look! No one speaks. A child's corpse is lying on the bottom of a cart. They are waiting for the police to come.

The newborn child has been found on a bed, with
a handkerchief stuffed in its mouth. Suffocated.
Who killed it? – Its mother did.

*   *   *

Long, slow, dark train. In the next compartment,
the sorry sight of five men in handcuffs under guard.
Do you know what it feels like to see men in chains
on their way to prison? The plainclothes escort
seems to have overheard the three Hail Mary's
which I was silently reciting for the prisoners.
He smiles. Speaks to me.
'You see that one?'
He points to one of the men asleep with his mouth
half-open and the light from the window glinting on
his handcuffs.
'He killed his wife to get rid of her and marry
someone else.'

*   *   *

Some friends invite me to debate with an anarchist
who has just arrived in town. I accept.
He is a tall young man with black hair. His pale
face ill accords with his shifty looks. I feel uneasy.
He begins talking about love and I listen mis-
erably. He argues for free love, divorce, adultery.
I feel as if I am suffocating under the avalanche of
obscenities. It seems hardly worthwhile to refute his
arguments. A gang of teddyboys guffaw and clap at
his more salacious sallies.

Love? – a combining of cells.
The sex act? – like blowing your nose.
Marriage? – the nastiest feature of Christianity.
The family? – medieval nonsense.

2. Through the Rhododendrons

I have got away from it all. I felt I had to. I left the
valley some hours ago and the sparkling stones of
the mule track winding ahead of me are interspersed
with patches of green. I am happy to be climbing.

Standing still for a moment, I look down at a
group of houses far below in the green gloom. Smoke
from their chimneys is forming clusters of white
flowers in the air, slowly dispersing against the
brown of the mountainside. Now I can hear the
churchbells and sharpen my pace to find a camp site
before it gets dark. The higher I climb, the lighter
my body and the easier the path become. I can't see
any details in the valley now. It's getting late.

The stream down below has turned to a shade of
violet.

I am hoping to spend the night in a shepherd's
hut.

*   *   *

In fact, I had to spend the night with the sheep. The

acrid smell of the animals clings to my thick coat next morning. Yes, I fell asleep with my head pillowed on a bundle of sticks. Near me lay a big ewe, which started licking its baby lamb in the middle of the night. They were happy, bound up in each other. The lamb blissfully closed its eyes and seemed to smile while the mother was licking it with her rough tongue. It seemed to me that though it loved her milk, it loved her caresses even more. Certainly these were more nourishing in effect. Dawn found me much further up. I felt as lithe and fresh as a mountain goat and so inclined to run that I had soon left last night's shepherd behind, who had kindly given me a bowl of milk.

Above me, a hawk is sharply etched against the blue. I think it is looking at me and assessing me as some odd and dangerous animal unfit to feed to its fledglings waiting up there on the crags. It wishes I were a large mole, a small rabbit or one of those tender little birds which can be snapped up in a sudden swoop. The dew shines on my well-greased boots.

When the sun rises over a distant peak, I kneel down on the track and pray.

'*Gloria in excelsis Deo!*'

How well I feel up here and how well I pray! I feel enveloped in God's love, like the lamb last night under its mother's calm and watchful eye.

Now the sun is beginning to make itself felt, warming away the shivers of earlier hours. I slow down and happily think that I shall soon be up among the rhododendrons. Then I shall see the high pastures, then the rocks, then the glaciers . . .

*   *   *

The rhododendrons are all round me now and I decide to stay here for the day. What a lovely place this is! I shall pass an enjoyable, reflective day half way up the mountain. I shall go on to-morrow. I need to think, and to think you don't have to be too tired.

I shall stop here.

The sky is so beautiful and the mountain is covered in flowers. It all seems specially designed so that I can take stock of myself. I can kneel down when I feel like doing so, I can shout my prayers at the top of my voice to God. I am alone with him, and round me lies a world speaking to me of him with potent tongue.

I am so happy that I am surprised to find myself crying with joy. My tears make sky and earth glitter more marvellously than ever. Looking at the distant mountains, I recite the psalms for Terce.

'I raise my eyes to the Mountain –
    where will help come from for me?
My help will come from the home of Yahweh
    who made heaven and earth.'

The roar of a far-away torrent accompanies my prayers.

*   *   *

I eat my lunch on the grass beside a spring. I lay out

the bread on a smooth stone. The sun is now inclining towards evening. It is the moment which St Basil called 'the hour of incense'.

The whole world now seems like a church for the Most High and I feel as though the creatures round me are bidding me pray. They want me to act as their interpreter. I am to put their dumb adoration into words. A black beetle stops near me and takes a look at me. It is evidently on its way home from work. Unseen, perhaps at the mouth of its burrow, its wife is on the lookout for its return. Between her legs, her children's little eyes are watching too.

This morning's hawk makes its last circle in the sky before nightfall.

The time has come. I kneel down and recite the psalms of Vespers.

'Like the Mountain of Zion
 are those who trust in Yahweh.
The Enthroned One of Jerusalem
 is never one to totter!'

The skies become misty. There is a sense of wonder in the air.

The beetle has disappeared into its burrow and the hawk has gone back to its nest. I think of last night's sheep and remember the rough tongue licking the lamb's white fleece. I have the sensation that the whole creation is a symphony of love, performed by an orchestra filling earth and sky.

I continue my devotions with Psalm 128.

'How blest, everyone who fears Yahweh,
   who walks in his ways!
You will indeed eat the fruit of your labours,
   happy and well-provided will you be:
like a fruitful vine, your wife,
   on the inner walls of your house;
Your sons round your table,
   like shoots round an olive-tree.'

I close the book and rest my head against the
rock. Before me a field of rhododendrons stretches
away into the distance and for the first time I see
them in their full magnificence.

The rhododendrons are as strong and lovely as
love, as delicate and tender as love. Pink, like
children's cheeks.

I gaze intently at them and imagine curious
shapes emerging from the twisted branches beneath
the masses of pink blossom. I see the corpse of a
dead child lying in a cart, then I see the face of that
woman under the streetlights of Genoa . . .

No, no, no!

The love of which all creation speaks to me is not
the same as this.

Away with you, horrible sight! Why, Man, have
you defiled it thus? Why do you not return to the
peaceful ways traced for you by your God?

The ways pursued by sheep, beetle and hawk?

Why only you astray?

Away with you, you visions of evil! Leave me to
contemplate the rhododendrons, leave me to bathe
in that harmonious song performed by an infinity of

artists under the face of heaven!

Leave me!

I take a book out of my rucksack – the Bible, my constant companion.

It is God's word, his letter written to men throughout the centuries: it is Truth. I open it at the first page, at the very beginning of the human epic, and start reading.

God said: 'It is not good than man should be alone. I shall make him a helpmate' (Gn 2:18).

I close my eyes, but the colours of the rhododendrons are still behind my eyelids.

So, love is God's will, I think, and a wife is decreed by his Wisdom!

Yes, look! 'So God made the man fall into a deep sleep. And while he slept, he took one of his ribs and enclosed it in flesh. And the rib which God had taken from the man, he built into a woman and brought her to the man' (Gn 2:21–22).

The blue of the sky is getting darker. Far off, the brilliant white of the glaciers stands out triumphantly against the other evening colours. Again I close my eyes. Before me, the pink of the rhododendrons melts into the blue of the sky, making it mild and warm.

I ponder over God's saying and the meaning of the hole made by God in Adam's flesh.

A hole, hence a void, a void throbbing with yearning, a lonely void, the very image of loneliness.

In Adam's flesh, very close to his heart, God excavated a loneliness, a loneliness yearning to be filled, a loneliness filling Adam with a new un-

'easiness, prompting him to seek that part of himself which is now outside him though still needed to complete his personality.

Yes, it is outside him, close beside him as he sleeps, and from it God is constructing a creature, woman, to whom Adam can in all truth say, 'You are bone of my bones and flesh of my flesh' (Gn 2:23).

And his sleep? What is the meaning of his deep sleep, while Almighty God is lovingly constructing this masterpiece?

Yes, I've got it! I know it! The sleep is ecstatic contemplation, the contemplation of a grandeur and gentleness such as only God can display and to which Adam contributes nothing except his admiration: God is doing all the work, while Adam is passive, as utterly passive as though asleep.

And God makes the cavity in Adam larger and larger and, with the cavity, desire, and the tension between him and what is part of him but yet outside him; and under God's hand, this becomes the object of his love, of his basic quest, of endless dialogue, and will be joined to him by a chain which, though invisible, is stronger than death and more forceful than a flood.

Night is coming on and the first star has appeared in the luminous sky.

Now I see God's plan and understand why human love is so powerful and so sweet.

I should like to keep quite still, so as not to lose the enchanting impact of this thought. Woman completes man, man completes woman: woman is complementary to man's personality, man is complementary to hers. Unity is achieved in this mysterious 'work' of God's, when man seeks woman as part of himself and in the ecstasy of love says, 'You are bone of my bones and flesh of my flesh.' Then that unity will be complete, and beautiful and fruitful and delightful and soothing, since willed by God.

And as this was so for Adam, so will it be for all men, so will it be for me. God's gifts are given without recall!

Isn't this so?

Haven't you ever felt the cavity near your heart? I have felt it often enough in the indescribable loneliness of the dreaming years. And it gets even stronger and its voice ever more insistant. Yes, God has dug a cavity near my heart, a cavity crying out to be filled. God can send me too into a deep sleep, a creative sleep . . .

And now I almost feel afraid — a miracle of some sort seems so likely to happen.

I feel so possessed by the truth of this that, if I were to reach out my hand, I should feel the hair of the creature I seek beneath my fingers. If I were to sit down, I feel that she would walk close past me. If I were to open my mouth and speak, she would be listening.

My heart begins beating faster. It seems such an overwhelming privilege to speak to the one whom I have dreamt of as a wife! To see the one who could be the mother of my children!

Yet everything round me urges me to do so. How

I should love to hear her speak, and tell her what I think about this symphony rising from earth to heaven and which in the first place came down from heaven to earth: I mean, love!

Why should I not? Now that there are all those stars in the sky . . .

*   *   *

Sitting down, I hear the rustle of her clothes.
I began talking to her; it was easy!
And what I said, I have written in this book.

3. What is Married Love?

'What is married love?' you asked me as you gazed into the distant valley, your now timid eyes skilfully evading mine.

How strange this timidity invading the virginal soul when talk turns to love; your heart seems to stop beating, a sweet unease fastens on the soul.

What is married love?

The sky was now full of stars and silence lay over all things.

It seemed as if I was talking to myself, and indeed I was talking to myself since you are me and I can't find a single word to say about myself without including you.

Listen!

Married love is the sweet image of God.

You know that God is a Trinity, that is to say, One in Three Persons.

Have you ever wondered why God is not One in One Person, but One in Three Persons?

God is One in Three Persons because he is Love:

the Father, the Son and the Holy Spirit.

The Father begets the Son from all eternity, contemplating him as the mirror of his own perfections and loving him with infinite love.

The Son, begotten by the Father, contemplates the Father as the Author of all things, loving him with infinite love.

Between the Father and the Son is a current of love, the Holy Spirit uniting the two Divine persons, being Substantial Love and the Third Person of the Holy Trinity.

The Three Divine Persons are but one single flame of love.

Married love, the family, is the sweetest image of the Trinity. Thus: husband, wife, son.

The husband chooses the wife, seeing her to be rich in those gifts which are dear to him: gentleness, beauty, charm – and loves her. The wife chooses the husband, seeing him to be rich in the gifts which she seeks: strength, stalwartness, thoughtfulness – and loves him. Between the two: the son, born of them both and uniting them with a chain surpassing earth and reflecting elements of eternity.

Love is a pale, yes, but sweet image of the Trinity.

Love is the model of the union between Christ and the Church

The Bible in its entirety can be thought of as a dramatic yet gentle conversation between Israel and God. And who is Israel, if not an image of the Church? And who is the Church, if not souls?

Hence, in the ultimate analysis, the Bible is a loving conversation between God and the soul considered as bride. In countless passages, God is called the bridegroom of the soul, and the *Song of Songs* celebrates this marital relationship most sublimely.

Listen, beloved sister, and see if you can find a finer declaration of love than this:

'Next time I saw you when I was passing, you had reached the age for love. I spread part of my cloak over you, covering your naked body. Then I plighted my troth to you and entered into an agreement with you – says the Lord Yahweh – and you became mine.

'Then I bathed you in water and anointed you with oil. I gave you brocaded dresses, fine leather shoes, and I fastened a fine linen belt round your waist and dressed you in lawn. For jewellery I gave you bracelets for your wrists and a necklace for your throat. I gave you a nose-ring and earrings and put a splendid diadem on your head' (Ezk 16:8–12).

Doesn't this exactly describe the attentions which Christ has lavished on us?

Our soul was poor and dressed in rags, wandering the streets of the world. Along comes the Divine Conqueror and, unconcerned about her poverty, makes her his.

And his love has never diminished since; his intimacy has filled our life.

Don't the delights of the Eucharist outdo any other kind of intimacy in intimacy? Isn't the conversation of a soul in union with God the most wonderful love-talk that ever could be imagined?

Listen to what the *Song of Songs* has to say about the intimate conversation between God and the soul:

'I hear my beloved.
   See how he comes
leaping on the mountains,
   bounding over the hills!
My beloved is like a gazelle,
   like a young stag!

'See where he stands
   behind our wall!
He is looking in at the window,
   he is peering through the lattice!

'My beloved speaks,
   this is what he says to me:
Come then, my love,
   my lovely one, come!' (2:8–10)

Can God's appeal to the soul be described in more lovingly urgent terms?
And this is the way the soul answers:

'I sleep, but my heart is awake.
   I hear my beloved knocking,' (5:2)

and goes to meet him with this cry:

'I am my beloved's,
   and his desire is for me!' (7:11)

And when she finds and is at rest with him, in that sweet intimacy she exclaims:

'O set me like a seal on your heart,
    like a seal on your arm,
for love is strong as Death,
    passion as enduring as Sheol.
Its flash is like the lightning,
    a very great flame indeed!
Were a man to offer all the wealth of his house
    to buy love, contempt is all he would purchase!'
(8:6–7)

Why does the Bible choose this simile?

Because married love is the most intimate form of union imaginable between human beings, a union in which our self-giving is as unconditional as it can be, in which the beloved is the complete object of our affections.

The Lord says: You are to love God with all your heart, with all your soul and with all your mind. Hence, no human relationship offers a profounder image of the commandment to love God than that which exists in married love. No loving relationship between father and son, between brother and sister, between friend and friend, demands as total a dedication as that of marriage. Here, the most unconditional dedication is the very basis of the relationship. And here again we find the finest language, the loveliest similes and the most definitive teaching on the relationship between the soul and God, between Christ and the Church.

Isn't this true?

When a man loves a woman, and vice-versa, he gives himself up to her. He wants to belong to her and wants her to belong to him.

Every kind of love, I agree, arouses the desire for reciprocation in us, but from the beloved we demand not merely reciprocation but that special sort of love in which the beloved belongs to me to the same degree as I for my part want to belong to my beloved.

This love, culminating in an individual union, in which two beings become a single being – that is to say, two in one flesh – lays the foundation for this close union and makes it possible.

Married love is the most significant of I-Thou relationships, and the cry issuing from both partners as though forced out of them, namely, 'I love you!' is without question the loveliest prayer that the soul can address to her God and certainly the sweetest answer that God's infinite love can make to the littleness of the human soul.

So isn't married love a fine thing, if God chose it to be the human model for the mystical life?

Married love is fruitfulness

Now, the divine element in married love is fruitfulness.

God is everlasting fruitfulness and his love creates the worlds and confers fruitfulness on these worlds.

Look at the soil: how fruitful it is in bringing forth life! Similarly, a woman's womb is fruitful in bringing forth life. But the soil, if it is to bring forth life, needs the sun, just as a woman, if she is to bring forth life, needs a husband.

What joy there is in fruitfulness! It is a very sharing in God's joy at being a Father!

This life-giving quality alone would be enough to raise marriage to giddy heights. For certainly there is no greater mystery in nature than the birth of a new creature endowed with an immortal soul, even though that soul is always bestowed by God!

But marriage is not fruitful only in that sense. It is fruitful in a way transcending child-bearing, being fruitful in a spiritual sense. Even if there are no children, marriage is important since in itself, by being a union, it corresponds to the express will of God: 'It is not good for man to be alone; I shall make him a helpmate.'

Puritans see the meaning of marriage exclusively in terms of procreation, regarding love as . . . well, as a necessary evil . . . which has to be endured if you want to have children. But the Catholic Church, the repository of Truth, thinks very differently and makes her children pray as follows: 'O Lord, who at the creation of mankind, by forming woman out of man revealed that they are a union of the flesh and of sweet love . . .'

That is what the Church says: 'sweet love' – and sweet love even if, by God's mysterious designs, the marriage is not to be blessed with the birth of children!

In a word, the union is fruitful in itself. It is spiritually fruitful. Spiritually fruitful by virtue of the warmth of the parties' mutual self-giving, spiritually fruitful by virtue of the incalculable influence which they have on each other, by virtue of the spiritual progress made possible by each for other through love, itself made easier by this particular way of living, and so forth. And lastly, it is fruitful because it helps husband and wife each to become complete personalities. Man becomes complete in marriage, he matures, learns to love more, learns to suffer more, understands things which he couldn't understand before. And the same thing is true for a woman who, once a mother, acquires a quality which she certainly never had in earlier days.

You agree?

But there is even more to it than that.

Married love is a source of holiness

Marriage in itself is holy, because willed by God. Remember God's commandment — for too many forget it! —

'A man must leave father and mother and cling to his wife, and the two become one body' (cf. Gn 2:24).

But it is even holier than this, Christ having raised it to the dignity of a sacrament, thus transforming it into a channel of grace.

Does anyone doubt that Baptism, Holy Communion, Holy Orders, are sources of grace? Why then not marriage too? It is a sacrament, just as much a sacrament as the others.

For Christian married love is transfigured by charity, that is to say, by love for our neighbour. The individual charm of the beloved is ennobled to the highest degree when expressing the eternal dignity of the soul as temple of the Holy Spirit. The love binding husband and wife grows stronger when each loves the other as a member of the Mystical Body.

What a sense of respect, of chastity, there is in married love when fully aware! And when you consider that this love is then transfigured into most lively zeal for the beloved's salvation, what can possibly still be lacking to fuse them both in even more burning charity, to help each other scale the life of perfection? When I reflect that I ought to feel responsible for your becoming holy, I burn with zeal and my soul fills with sacred terror in case my own unworthiness should hinder you.

And lastly, has not Christ himself said: 'Where two are united in my name, I shall be with them'? That means us. That will be our family and he will be there with us, because we shall be united in his name.

Can marriage have a more exalted dignity if two creatures unite not only to raise their souls to God but to form an intimate fusion with Christ to glorify the Lord by their existence? And can it have a more exalted dignity when this touching, luminous, pure married affection allows husband and wife to feel like one heart-beat in Christ?

*   *   *

So aren't we right to conduct a holy crusade for the true appreciation and sublimation of this wonderful design of God's, called the family? Especially today, with a more mature laity, aren't we right to suggest new themes to engage their spirituality?

To help them by every possible means to fulfil such a basic human vocation?

4. A Prayerdesk for Two

Three stars have guided my path.

They appeared in my firmament as and when God decreed, and shone so brightly that I never doubted why they were there.

One star guided my childhood, another my youth and the third appeared when I was on the threshold of manhood.

The childhood star was my family and had two golden rays: my father and my mother.

My father was a strong, taciturn man. After work he would take me for walks beside the River Po, where I used to amuse myself catching cockchafers under the beech leaves and organising naval battles in the irrigation ditches.

He would look on silently. Only later did he learn to talk to me and tell me how much he loved me.

Then, when I left home, he felt lonely, almost panic-stricken, and when I came home, he would become talkative and calm again.

My mother brought all the poetry of her homeland to my childhood.

She was always singing and had a fine ringing

voice which I could immediately recognise when I was in church serving Mass.

When I looked round, she would be looking at me; I would look at her, we would smile at each other and feel happy.

One Christmas, at midnight, while we children were all in church, she gave birth to our sixth baby brother as our Christmas present and when, three years later, death tried to take him from us, I would see her watching over him night and day to keep him safe, enduring until his final spasm that long, monotonous wail, never to leave her memory or ours: Ah! Ah! Ahhh!

*   *   *

The star of adolescence was the apostolate, and this was how I discovered it . . .

I had met a young doctor who was already making a name for himself for his brains and kind heart. Being with him was a delight. He was clear-eyed, with an iron will.

He used to tell us laymen that we had to be saints. We had to conquer the whole world for Christ.

Seeing him at the hospital in his white jacket, I used to think that this was exactly what a modern monk ought to be like. And in fact, just like a monk, he taught me to say the Little Hours of our Lady and used to recite them with me in the public gardens outside the hospital.

At his wish, and full of enthusiasm, I joined the junior section of Catholic Action. This was the most vigorous Christian youth organisation of its day.

Within a month of joining, I had the nerve to throw myself into the fray. 'Luigi tells me you ought to be in the propaganda department,' Bardelli the engineer said to me one day; he was in charge of the outlying districts of our diocese, Turin.

'In propaganda? Me? But I've never done any public speaking!' I replied, appalled.

'My dear chap, you'll soon learn, don't worry! This Sunday, you will go to Casanova. There you will find about two hundred country people. You will talk to them about the encyclical on Charity. Alright?'

'Yes, alright! You give the orders, I obey them – but . . . you take full responsibility if things go wrong.'

I had a week in which to get ready. I spent it preparing a polished written address and practising it in front of a mirror, so as to give a really professional performance.

On the Sunday, I went over the well-memorised phrases in my head as I sped along to my mission-field in a third-class carriage.

When I got to the station, I was met by a young man about six foot tall, who instantly singled me out and said, 'You must be Carretto? Come along. I'm to take you out to the meeting,' and made me hop into a buggy. After nearly an hour's drive through the countryside, we arrived at Casanova, where a few minutes later I found myself in a dusty little hall presiding over a gathering of country people waiting to hear what I had to say.

Now came the acid test and I began pretty well
. . . but at a given moment my words ceased to flow,
I got in a muddle and lost the thread . . .

My brow broke out in a cold sweat. A thick mist
danced over the close-cropped heads of the country
people listening in silence to my efforts as a speaker.

I don't know what I said. I shall never know.
Eventually, I seemed to hear someone applauding to
encourage me, so that I shouldn't burst into tears
. . . I don't know what I said. I shall never know. But
that night, going back to the station in the buggy
with all the young people from the Youth Association scrambling into it, wanting to come with me . . .
and we sang . . . and the stars shone . . . and in the
sky I remember having seen that second star which
was to guide my life: the apostolate.

And, as my throat contracted in sweetest anguish,
the star spoke to me and said, 'You too, yes, you
too.'

To me it sounded like the voice of the ages, of
Paul, of Benedict, of Francis Xavier, reaching me to
rouse and transform me.

Look, it said to me, so far you have thought that
being a Christian meant going to church services so
as not to upset mother. But now you must grasp that
being a Christian means being an apostle, a missionary, means go, go, go.

From that evening onwards, beloved, it was all go.

The ideal had seized on me and, with other wonderful, ardent companions, I no longer knew how to
stop. I never stayed at home of an evening, no longer
appeared on the football ground of a Sunday.

I had to keep going . . . I think (and it would be interesting to work it out as a spiritual phenomenon) that if I were to total up the number of miles covered today by members of the lay apostolate, it would far exceed the distances covered by missionary endeavours regarded as more important.

And as I went . . . I came to know the third star. And this is how:

I had to keep going . . .

I arrived in a town in Piedmont. I had just been conducting ten meetings in a row and was very tired. It was late.

A wind blowing off the mountains made me shiver at the thought of the cold sheets in the seminary where I was to spend the night. But instead? A wonderful invitation from a very old friend whom I happened to run into in the street.

'Come on. We'll have a nice evening together. I want you to meet my wife.'

I didn't need asking twice and spent an enchanted evening at my friend's. The warmth revived me completely. A first-rate dinner made me forget the hardships of the day. The conversation moved me profoundly.

What marvellous things I heard, sitting with these two wonderful people, who thought of their marriage as a gift from Mary Immaculate. What freshness, what purity of thought what poetry!

They really believed in love and drank it drop by drop as a gift from God.

After supper, they took me into their bedroom

and there I saw something I had never yet seen in any married couple's room: a prayerdesk for two.

They used to say their prayers together.

For a split second, looking at that little bit of wooden furniture at the foot of the bed, I glimpsed the rebirth of the rising generation. They had new things to say, strong words, decisive words, words of complaint, of protest, of revolt.

This, this was what the life of the Christian laity should be like, this was the new poetry, this was the new masterpiece to be built, this was the new holiness to be achieved!

When we came out and went back into the living-room, we found ourselves in agreement on the subject that needed sorting out: what sort of prayer-life should be recommended to two young married people who intended to live their married life as a form of consecration?

We discussed this at length and then having reached our joint conclusion wrote down the mutual obligations on two sheets of paper. One was put on their prayerdesk, and the other I kept. This is what it says:

'On waking up and on the striking of the hour, have we recited the basic prayer: *Pater, non mea voluntas sed tua fiat*?

'Have we practised the threefold morning obligation of Meditation, Mass and Holy Communion? Have we venerated Mary Most Holy by reciting the Rosary?

'Have we consoled Jesus suffering throughout history by visiting the Blessed Sacrament, by bearing our own sorrows with fortitude and by affording relief to the sorrows of others?

'Have we been industrious, good-humoured, honest and quiet at our work?

'Have we prayed for our dead?

'Have we improved our minds by studying the Holy Scriptures?'

*   *   *

When I left that night, the wind was still blowing off the mountains. Gleaming in the moonlight, the Alps seemed to be asleep. The town was deserted and my footsteps were muffled by the snow. It was certainly very cold out of doors but, looking up into the sky, I then saw my third star.

It seemed to be smiling down on me and my happy tears made it shine all the lovelier, all the brighter.

5. The Family as a Model of the Church

We were sitting down when the day was at its hottest. It was that same time of day when Jesus once sat tired at the well-head, waiting for the Samaritan woman, while his disciples were away in the town buying food. The time of day when people make for home.

Jesus no longer had a home. He had renounced his. 'Foxes have holes and the birds of the air have nests, but the Son of Man has nowhere to lay his head' (Mt 8:20).

Jesus no longer had a home. He had renounced his because everyone couldn't have one. And how bitter the words must have sounded, 'Even the foxes . . .'!

Perhaps he was thinking of the happy days of his adolescence when he too had a home. It was a poor home, but his own. Besides, his mother was there! And she would support his fair head in her lap while she told him the history of his people and caressed him with the gentleness that all mothers have. Jesus had renounced all this and now recalled it as a warning to those who wanted to follow him. Per-

haps he was thinking back over the hours punctu-
ated by Joseph the Carpenter's hammer, while
between one job and the next he thought about
leaving the nest, like a bird once its feathers
are grown.

Undoubtedly he was thinking about his home, as
he sat on the coping of the well with his feet covered
in dust and the sweat clinging to his clothes after his
long walk.

How gladly he would have hurried back to see his
home again! . . . But that was a temptation. . . . He
had renounced his home because other people did
not have one.

*   *   *

Yes, one fit to live in.

One worthy of a human being, a home partly
made up of a man, as it were, and even more so of a
woman. A home in which to be born, in which to
laugh, to cry, to love: a home where memories ac-
cumulate and where their perfume clings to your
clothes and never goes away, never, like something
holy.

A home worthy of a human being!

Some time ago I was in a town in Southern Italy
and took a walk through the poorer streets to see
how the people lived.

This was the sort of life I saw. A dark, dank, dirty
alley. The houses of the poor opened onto this. The
priest who was taking me round and knew the district well said, 'Do you see that? There are fourteen

people living in that room. Ten in this one. And so on.'

And I said, 'But how can so many people sleep in one room at night?'

'How do they manage? They lay mattresses on the floor – the only poor wealth of the household – and there they go to sleep in a welter of bodies.'

I was saddened at the thought of the way these poor people lived. What terrible things might not happen in this sort of situation! The least of which was incest!

No, Jesus renounced his own home because so many people could not have one. And people in positions of power ought to feel this, and Christians ought to grasp this, and everyone ought to take action to safeguard human dignity.

We were talking about love, but how can love thrive in such surroundings? Love is a plant which needs taking care of, which needs thoughtfulness, intimacy, breathing-space.

There are words which should be spoken in privacy, there are caresses which require a certain modesty and should be exchanged in private, where not even mother is there to see.

How sorry we ought to feel for poor people burdened with fatigue, with the endless struggle for their daily bread and with no home, this being worst of all. It is bearable to work all day, one is prepared, especially when one is young, to have children, to sweat at achieving something and at making something of oneself, but to come home in the evening and not find any privacy or peace, not be able to hold a private conversation with your wife, not to be able to take her in your arms and tell her that you have been thinking of her all day, is really inhuman.

I never felt so disgusted by rich people as when I began to understand the human heart.

And I never felt so much joy as the day when, faced with a young friend who wanted to get married but had nowhere to live, I took my courage in both hands and went to see an old lady who had a twelve-bedroom house and said, 'Mrs X . . .; in the name of Jesus Christ, do this charitable deed: give three small rooms in your house to two lovely people who want to get married. Make two people happy!'

Do you know, the lady agreed? She had another door made in her frontage and took the two young people in.

Such are the Christians of our times: very different from the old dragons of last century in black dresses with buttoned-up collars, who used indeed to take gruel up to the garret but handed it over with a lengthy moral lecture, interspersed with umpteen questions about the poor family's comings and goings. If everyone with large unused premises would do as much, what a lot of new families would be able to set up house!

And surely grace, bringing with it that life welling up behind the smile of God the Creator, would redound on the heads of the givers.

What a blissful thing a good home is!

Jesus gave up his own because everyone could not have one.

*   *   *

You ask me what sort of home I should like?

At the question, my mind is flooded with memories of the homes in which I have lived and which I found desirable.

As a boy, I was impressed by my grand-parents' home. I loved it and couldn't have asked for anything better.

It was a big old country house, where my father had been born. It had a complete world inside it, like an abbey: from the bakery where they baked the bread to the huge, very high bed which I could reach only by climbing on a chair.

It was really impressive, that bed – like a monument. And when I was little, I could hide under the quilts when my mother came looking for me.

Then there was the sheepfold with the sheep, the barn with the farm-workers' implements, the cool, dark cellar, the drawing-room always kept shut up with the portraits of our ancestors in their awe-inspiring side-whiskers, the store-room with its fruit, and then the cats and dogs and chicken and all that well-loved world smelling so wholesomely of bread and earth – this I can never forget.

It was good.

And it was good because my grandmother had broken with that very bad custom by which the family lived as a tribe – the patriarchal family in which the newly married went on living with the older generation, having no independence or authority of their own.

It may have been socially and economically necessary, but certainly it was not good.

And I have never been able to understand how such a way of living can find romantic souls ready at the drop of a hat to hymn its glories: Oh for the good old days! Oh for the fine old patriarchal family!

If they had read their Bible properly, they would know what God thought about it. This is what God has to say: 'This is why a man must leave father and mother, and cling to his wife, and the two become one body.'

'Must leave' says the Scripture, which means that he has to make a new home, tear himself away, acquire his own property, exert his own authority.

In this respect at least, the young people of today have shown themselves more resourceful and more obedient to God's command.

And how right they are!

Everything brought to birth is a seedling being transplanted, and the transplant has to be complete, even if it does cause pain.

If God has commanded thus, this is what is right. He knows.

*   *   *

From then on, between the two extremes, my desires were to oscillate between all sorts of different kinds of home. Big ones, little ones, town ones, country ones, serious-minded ones, jolly ones, romantic ones or classical ones, depending on the moment and the changeable tastes of youth.

Now, if I had to put all this in a nutshell, I should be perfectly content with, and should serenely put

my trust in, two factors, the one grim, the other
cheerful, which characterise the times in which it
has been given me to live: that is to say, the
harshness of the economic situation, and the good
taste shown by our contemporaries in the way they
design their homes.

The harshness of the times is an accident of fate
and nothing is served by worrying about that, for
fear we increase our own crosses which are
numerous and heavy enough already. We must do
all we can to make things better, then smile and go
on in the thought that no one can take away our
peace of heart.

Good taste in modern housing cannot be disputed
and greatly contributes to the peace of mind of
young married couples. The walls may be on the
thin side, but then young couples have a lot to say
quietly to each other – and whispers can't be
overheard.

So we take the house as we find it, but whatever
else it hasn't got, it must have two things: a door
and a window.

A door first of all, to shut the rest of the world out.
With a key, to be sure. To shut out strife, torment,
incomprehension, all day if possible. But at least in
the evening, so that you can rest your weary head on
the breast of someone who does understand and has
chosen to scale life's mountain with you.

A door, sometimes to shut out even my own kith
and kin. That seems hard, but has to be done, especially in matters concerned with the children's
upbringing. Plenty of relations would like to meddle

in this, by spoiling them, giving them presents and fussing over them.

And a window. A fine window with a view of the sky, so that I don't forget about my home above. A fine window often to stand in front of with you to recite the Preface of the Dead: 'Lord, life is changed, not taken away; and this earthly dwelling is destroyed, while you are preparing one in heaven.'

Wouldn't you like that?

If we could have anything else as well as a door and a window, it would be nice to have a small terrace, four pots of flowers, a little study, two delightful features? All the better, we'll take it! But if these aren't part of the deal, we shall go on smiling, since the greatest thing of all, which no one can take away, is love.

*   *   *

For, you see, for me my home is a church.

And our home will be a church. A church where people love and sanctify each other, where people suffer, are born, and pray.

And in it we shall talk very quietly, peacefully, serenely.

And then, as in church, there will be pictures: of our dead.

And, as in church, we shall begin the day by praying together. Above all, meditating together.

This is the plan which I should like to put into practice with you:

We sit down while the house is still quiet and offer

God the first half hour of the day, meditating together on the things of God, contemplating his mysteries and waiting for the strength required for the labours of the day.

Then we set out for the larger church outside, to receive Jesus. This must always be a fixed point in our plans: frequent, perhaps daily, communion.

And when this is impossible for both of us because of pressure of work or because of having to look after the children, then at least one of us will go and, having received the Eucharist, will hurry home at top speed so as to bring Christ palpitating within the walls of our house. And if there are children, these should kiss the breast of the communicant in the fervent desire of becoming living tabernacles themselves.

But the real time for intimacy will have to be the evening.

I know that the apostolate doesn't leave many evenings free and I shall often have to resign myself to this; all the same, these evenings out will only be the unavoidable ones since the tug of the sweet church in miniature will draw us back to the intimate life we so love.

To give you a clearer idea of the way I should like to live, let me describe life in a truly Christian home, the life of one of my dearest friends who succeeded in creating the sort of family we are dreaming of. His name was Peppino Rovera.

Listen!

He and his family lived . . . well, never mind

where. They were devoted to one another. Each day was one long affirmation of love.

But the time of day which I used to find most moving was the evening. In the living room of that house, conversation flowered with a marvellous freshness and level-headedness.

They would read the Bible, talk about the apostolate, discuss social conditions and how to put them right; they dreamed of making a new world. Frivolous remarks were out of the question; idle gossiping found no takers. It wasn't a sitting-room – it was a church.

And grace gushed forth as though from a clear spring, and to see Peppino Rovera, the father, sitting in an armchair after a hard day's work – and really hard work too – with his two sons, one on his right, the other on his left with their arms round his neck, and the little girl gazing up at him at his feet, was the most spellbinding sight in the world.

If these children had anything to worry about, it was the thought of one day having to leave this close-knit home. For they all truly thought of themselves as a single entity: she part of him and the children part of the mother and father. No one had secrets from anyone else. To whom could they confide them, if not to one another. Where were they to seek solutions to the problems rising in their young souls, if not from their father and mother?

And when it grew late and when, notwithstanding the children's efforts to keep awake, their eyelids began to droop, Peppino would give the signal in his cheerful, ringing voice. In a matter of moments, the sitting-room had turned into a chapel.

Kneeling on the carpet in front of the table, which was now transformed into a shrine with all the photographs of their dead arranged round the statues of Jesus and Mary, they would say their prayers together.

This epitomised the whole day – this conversation with the Eternal, in a choir consisting of the living, of the angels, and of the dead outside under the stars.

If you had looked up at that moment, you would certainly have seen the heavens open and caught sight of the invisible. You would have glimpsed the shining wall of the heavenly home awaiting this family after the destruction of the earthly dwelling. Their father led the prayers. First came the fixed formulae, then the ever-varying prayers about the day just over and what had happened in it. Then it was the turn of the children or of the mother to make up and offer their prayers: a mixture of petitions, confessions, pleas for forgiveness and acts of adoration – a truly personal conversation with God.

No one was forgotten; and the dead and living known to the household were remembered in this little praying community, mentioned by name and bound together by the golden thread of love.

Then Peppino Rovera, sitting very straight, would bless his children one by one, making a little sign of the cross with his thumb on each forehead: truly God's representative in his own household.

This family – a church in miniature!

How often over the years my mind has gone back

to the first occasion when I saw them, and today
when he is no more and his children, having grown
up faithful to his schooling, themselves have their
own dreams to achieve – since little sparrows with
no nests must make new nests, new little churches
even lovelier, even holier – I can appreciate the value
of what he was doing.

Poor yet great was Peppino Rovera!

He was so devoted to his calling as father and husband that he looked on it as a consecrated life. And
thanks to his good example, I now understand the
sort of revolution which we young people must make
as we prepare for marriage.

We are through with thinking of marriage as a
second-rate kind of life. We are through with passing such a vital matter over in silence. Enough of all
that!

The family – a church in miniature!

A rebirth is on the way!

And when God in his inscrutable designs called
Peppino Rovera to himself and the time came for
him to utter the last *fiat* of resignation, this was the
testament he wrote:

'Do you want to know the recipe for concord, for
harmony, for unity and for peace in the home?
Every evening say your prayers together. All
together is the way.

'I am not giving you an order. Orders · are
irksome. This is a secret too sweet to be lightly
forgotten. Be faithful to this if you want to be happy.

'Furthermore: be charitable, every day of your

life. Study to be so with special delicacy of heart in times of trial and tribulation. This will give peace to your soul and evil will then have no power over you.

'And now I shall tell you something else.

'The times of anxiety and tears will not last forever. A father cannot die more than once; destruction and war must eventually have an end.

'A better kind of future is on the way.

'Enjoy it, I say, but remember: always respect the Law of God.'

Doesn't this read like a page from the Old Testament, about the Patriarchs? Doesn't it remind you of Jacob blessing his sons?

And so great was Peppino Rovera's influence that his two sons were each to lay a written note in their father's coffin.

I often think of those two pieces of yellowing paper on Peppino's corpse, perhaps with the handwriting still legible.

One said: 'Better die than sin.' And the other: 'Father, I shall work for Christ as you did.'

What finer reward could you have at the end of your life?

6. Intimacy

I once knew a professor who was frightened of emotion. He claimed not to be able to remember what his wife's kisses were like. I don't think he had ever kissed her, except perhaps on their honeymoon.

Shut in on himself, he considered any display of affection as a form of weakness, and intimacy as an intrusion. Childish nonsense, childish nonsense, he would say; he locked himself up in his study and lived like a lonely bear.

*   *   *

When I was a boy, I lived for a while with a childless married couple in the country. They used to send me down to collect the milk, made me wash the lemon containers in the evening and sent me to bed without kissing me goodnight.

I used to amuse myself with the dog, which got on much better with me than they did, licking my hands and, when it could, my face with its warm, wet tongue. Apart from the dog, I was terribly bored in that house. The couple had given up talking to each other. If he was in the garden, she was in the sitting-room; if she was in the garden, he was in the loft. They were good, regular people, went to Mass, were never unpleasant to each other and yet . . . how distant, how cold they were!

When they went out for a walk, he used to walk three paces ahead. I never once saw them arm in arm together. I never chanced on them sitting side by side talking to one another, paying a compliment or telling a joke.

Once, he went off on business and stayed away from the house for about six months. In those six months, he only sent one postcard. And that stayed for ages, poked under the glass top of the sideboard with these words written on it: 'Hope you are well – Remember to pay the rates – See about harvesting the maize – P.B.'

When he came back, she was in the sitting-room and I was stroking the cat.

Said she: That you?

Said he: Yes.

And taking his jacket off because it was a hot day, he went into the dining-room to have a glass of wine.

You understand, Beloved, that this home was not a little church but a little bear's cave, which I would not wish on a dog.

Union in marriage is not merely a physical union. Intimacy of heart, care for others' feelings, are integral parts of that union, contributing to it by giving a bit of joy and by helping each to endure the trials of life.

Love is not so much a body as a heart, not so much a heart as an unending conversation; it is a net growing ever tighter, establishing ever sweeter and more intimate bonds, out of which life's tapestry is woven.

Don't you agree?

Today we have to steer our course between two extremes: the permissiveness of the all too many, and the harshness of generations of country-folk who regard any show of affection as weakness. Both are wrong. The former debase love into sensuality, reducing relationships to physical impressions, thus poisoning the heart; the latter, uneducated as they are, shun conversation as a waste of time, shut themselves up in themselves and are often cruel to their wives, who need love and gentleness far more than they do food.

What a lot the apostolate can achieve in this sector!

Alas, there aren't enough teachers to go round.

The family rarely acquits itself of its mission, the school virtually never intervenes and the parish normally passes everything over in silence. So it comes about that the young learn the language of love from pop-songs, and their first conversations on this delicate topic are nearly always nothing but smutty talk, prompted by unwholesome curiosity and culminating in impure acts.

I should like you to read a few relevant pages written by two young people who really understood about love, Joseph Ollé-Laprune, a French diplomat, and his wife Alice Gavoty. The extracts have been taken from their diary.[1]

1 Published in the volume *Legami immortali* edited by Alice Gavoty, A.V.E., Rome.

I think the tone adopted by these two young
Christians is exactly right.

Listen:

August 11 – We have fused our two souls into one, the
better to lose this single soul in unconditional love
for the Lord, from whom and through whom our
love was born ... Nothing frightens me now,
whatever may betide, since by means of you, the
Lord has given me great strength and great peace
... What can conquer death itself, if not the love
with which I press you to my heart in tenderest
warmth of respect and gratitude!

August 17 – I, like you, am firmly convinced that our
affection not only will not be an obstacle to our loving God, but that we can fulfil our vocation of absolute love for God only through our love for one
another. Every moment I experience the truth of
this: that a true assent to God is conditional on our
love willed by Him, and this is why our love prompts
us to sacrifice everything to His love.

I know that by drawing closer to you I see all my
duties in clearer perspective and that through you I
have more strength to discharge them better.

Rome, April 2 – In Rome we were apart as little as
possible. Almost every day we went to Mass at S.
Bernardo's. We always made our communions
together and from the outset made a habit of making
our communions for the same intentions.

Nearly every evening I used to go and wait for him in S. Andrea della Valle, where there was a service at eight o'clock, and then we used to take a taxi up to the Quirinale to watch the sun setting behind St. Peter's, which I loved so much.

And it was always with the same joy that we retired into our bedroom, free at last from the continuous obligations of the day. He was very happy. He used to sing *Parsifal* and *Die Meistersinger* to me. And he made me take a tiny snail out of the Trappists' garden at the Catacombs, which then went to Paris with some lilies sent to Pierre and was then sent back by Renee in the diplomatic bag. As we hadn't got time to go to the Catacombs again and put it back among its flowers, Joseph, who wanted it to have a 'monastic setting', decided that I should take care of it until we left for Camaldoli, where we left it among the wild strawberries out in the woods near the Chapel of St. Romuald. Loreta, when I sent her to fetch the little creature a lettuce leaf, gravely said, 'It is clear that Your Excellency will make a good mother.'

From the start we used to say our prayers together, as well as a chaplet of the rosary, to which he was extremely attached.

Some evenings when I was tired after long duty-dinner-parties, I could have wished not to do so much, but he would never consent to this. We found the Lord more and more in each other, and we regarded this as the blessing on our union, which he had willed. Near Joseph, I almost always had an actual sense of God's presence. One day when I confided to him that I now felt much nearer to God than when we had got married, his eyes lit up with joy and he said, 'That is exactly what I want to be for you. I want you to know that I respect you as much as I love you, and that is saying everything. For me you are no other than the envoy of the Lord.'

June 29 – This morning we went to St. Peter's, where Monsignor Rocchi celebrated Mass for us in one of the sacristy chapels. Many a time and slowly have we crossed the space between the Confessio and the sacristy, having walked the same way last year after the Mass celebrated for us on St. Peter's tomb. 'That day, the Lord himself betrothed us,' he used to say, 'make no doubt about that!'

He used to talk of the union of our souls and lives as a union established by God himself and hence eternal, unchanging, without interruption being possible, ever more intimate, ever more perfect until its final fusion in heaven. He would say, 'Two in one for a lifetime is wonderful, and in your company how lovely, Beloved!'

We understood each other better every day, and our joy in being 'wedded together' as he put it, kept growing greater all the time.

He used to say, 'It's too wonderful having you as my wife. Do you know the joy, the security, the support that you mean for me? Over and over again at the Embassy, I remind myself that you are mine and that this surpasses the highest bliss that I ever believed the world could hold. I go into raptures at the thought that you are mine for ever. What would happen to us if we had to be separated now? You are the better half of me.'

He used to confide his doubts to me, his aspirations, his hopes, everything that he dreamed of achieving in the course of his work.

And I can still hear him saying in ringing tones, 'All that it involves notwithstanding, and despite everything that can happen, I can truthfully say that I am glad to be alive.'

That 'I am glad to be alive' rang out like a chime of bells. He said it twice and his eyes shone. That was in the Via San Vitale at about 4 o'clock under a blazing sun.

We had come out of the Collegio Angelico where we had been to confession together, which he liked doing. He wanted to do everything together and was never happier than when we thought of the same thing at the same moment. And since receiving absolution was a great joy for his great faith, he wanted us to receive this together.

Many an afternoon we went to the Collegio Angelico together for this reason, before going to the Embassy or paying calls.

This shared life of the soul was a help at every minute of the day. We thought that the Communion of Saints must take a special form through two souls sacramentally united and having all things in common.

Often, on Sundays, we used to go to St. Paul's or to the Catacombs of St. Callixtus and talk to old Fr. Bonaventura under the cypress trees.

Camaldoli July 12 – We spent a wonderful time working together even though we didn't have time to talk, but were so happy being near each other all the time that this in itself was a party. He said, 'Isn't this wonderful! Here we can be together even more than in Rome. Working together is a delight. I work so well when you are here. You make me serene and secure. I no longer get that unpleasant feeling of not being able to get done in time. You make everything seem easy. You are my peace, my dearest peace.'

At 7 a.m. we went to Mass with the hermits and that was the best moment of the day. We communicated at the same altar, as is the custom there, and after Mass went for a brisk walk in the forest, like children let out of school. This was our recreation. He took my hand and we ran together in the cool morning air under the pine trees. As usual, on coming back, we ran into the postman who had just brought us a bundle of letters. Another bundle arrived later.

September 19 – 'I foresee the time when our correspondence, through our exchanges of letters, will also become a sensible contact of souls. I love you so tenderly. Aren't you perhaps as completely and unreservedly mine as I am limitlessly yours?'

And his tenderness grew greater day by day, like mine, and I used to tell him how delicious it was to love each other so much. He would smile and say, 'Come on, tell me, aren't you just putting up with me? Do you really and truly love me?' And not giving me time to answer, would gently stroke my hair and go on, 'For my part, you see, my great love for you is ever new, ever stronger, ever more tenderly ardent, lifting me up like a wave. You know, you are my bliss and my life, that you are all my dreams come true, that you mean everything to me. I love you. I love you. I want to clothe you in tenderness. You are everything I have ever wanted, and more. It is an intoxicating joy to have you as a wife, to feel that for all eternity you and I shall be one. You are my life, my entire life. Do you understand what I am trying to say? And when I think that you might leave me, that you might die before me, I think I might go mad. I shouldn't be able either to work or to live. But you are here, my sweet peace. My whole heart thrills when I look at you; from afar I call to you when I am in pain, in temptation, in doubt. I tell myself that you are mine and this surpasses every joy I ever thought possible. I am all unreservedly yours. Even when you are far away, I feel your dear hand in mine, your heart beating in my breast, and then I am happy, so happy, and tell myself that this will never end . . . Then I close my eyes, since others cannot see the sudden light. I love you – I think I have the right to tell you so – as very few other women have been loved, as a universal principle of good. I am proud of loving you like this!' – And in his tenderness he always found new ways of touching my heart. He used to say, 'It is so lovely because it is so pure, so purifying.'

La Valbonne December 19 – 'How deeply I pine for you and how slow time is in passing . . . Now that these three weeks have come to an end — three very healthy, completely military weeks, but spent so far away from you and about which I have such a lot to tell you — how tenderly, how sweetly and tenderly I take you in my arms — in imagination — once again to say a most deeply felt "thank you." '

La Valbonne December 20 — '. . . Until tomorrow, Beloved. Words cannot express how much I want to see you.'

These last two letters, delayed in the post, arrived in Lyons after he did. Reading them, I was momentarily overcome. He smiled. Then said, 'Are you glad I love you so much? But look here, this is nothing; the poor words I have written are nothing in comparison with what lives in my heart and fills it to overflowing. And you know I love you in the name of the Lord! . . .'

December 23 — We left for Grenoble. Now that he was sure he was going to the front and would be going as a machine-gunner in an infantry regiment, he would have liked to spend a few days with me. He thought he would have another two or three weeks. He made plans, talked about Midnight Mass, and I was afraid all the time that we might be disappointed. Even so, his optimism overcame my fears and on arrival at the Hotel Moderne I unpacked his things for the short stay which he had planned for us there.

At 11 o'clock he came back from the depot and I asked him, 'Did everything go alright? Was the C.O. nice to you?' He didn't answer. He drew me to

him, laid his head on my shoulder and whispered
almost inaudibly, 'Are you going to be brave? I've
got to leave tonight.'

We had accepted everything, but not this, not
this. This ordeal was annihilating. Forlornly
clutching one another, sobbing helplessly together,
we cried like two children. He was the first to pull
himself together and, putting his hands on my
shoulders – a habitual gesture of his – said, 'We
must be very generous to God, in giving him what he
asks of us.' I am sure he could see the suffering in my
eyes. He was afraid that my will would not be as
strong as his and a look of anxiety flashed across his
face. He said, 'You will it all, don't you? Oh, tell me
that you do!' But he had misconstrued what I was
thinking. I couldn't feel any other way than he did.
Yvonne's words came to my lips, 'Yes, I will all,
everything that can make your own soul beautiful.'
He was intensely glad to know that our souls were so
at one at this moment. We looked at each other in
deepest, sweetest joy, in the knowledge that our love
was indeed the 'foundation of holy strength' which
he had wanted it to be, and that, supporting each
other, we should with all our soul give the Lord
this last terrible thing which he was asking of us.

Intent as always on being faithful to grace and on
making God what he called 'a good sacrifice' – he
hadn't got it in him to make any other kind – he
repeated, 'We are really willing, aren't we, Beloved?
We truly will whatever God wills, without reserva-
tion, with all our strength of soul?'

Then in each other's arms, in a trust surpassing

all words, together we offered his life as a burnt-offering. I do not know how we could have done that: presumably because our love was so strong. Beside him, in the enthusiasm of his heart, nothing, absolutely nothing, was impossible. The following February 18, when I knew that everything was over for us on earth, I felt that there was nothing more to be added to the sacrifice offered in his arms on December 23.

*   *   *

Don't you think, Beloved, that we should want to act like that? Feel like that? Love like that?

7. Watch and Pray

I was told that all men were sick because original sin had wounded human nature – but I took no notice.

I was told that I too was sick, having inherited the blood of the first sick man, Adam, from my father and mother – but I wasn't aware of it.

Experience convinced me that it was true.

First one sore appeared, then another, then another.

I tried to cure them by washing them in earthly water, earthly oil, earthly medicine, with no result.

Instead of healing up, the sores grew larger and deeper.

Then, from the Church, I learned that to get better I needed the water, the oil, the medicine of Heaven. I went in search of the medicine of Heaven and wanted to get better so badly that I found it.

I got it from a doctor who had come from Heaven and was called Christ.

One day, I met him on my way: alive, beautiful, fascinating as ever.

I asked him for medicine to heal my sores and he gave me his own Blood; I asked him for water to bathe my wounds and he gave me the water from his Side; I asked him for strength to get better and he gave me his Flesh.

I drank his Blood, I ate his Flesh and got better, or at least I began getting better.

He told me that I ought to go on with the cure until I died, since the evil was so deep that I should never make a complete recovery, having retained the terrible legacy of my first forefather's illness as a physical fact inside me.

Thenceforth I have been eating and drinking Christ, and thenceforth have continued to get better.

It is difficult to tell and list all the ills of human life: sin has upset it so much that we need all our resources to re-establish order in it.

Like a tremendous duel between an all-powerful remedy – God's blood, for example – and some deadly blood-poisoning surging up from the levels of sin and trying to invade the entire organism.

O divine medicine of Christ, you will accompany me to the end, so that I shall remember that I am a man who without you can do nothing.

*   *   *

If this is true for me, if this is true for you, Sister, it is easy to grasp the reality of human weakness!

Beware of forgetting it!

Our poor human nature is so threatened that, if we were not continually and sternly on the watch, we should never be able to achieve anything and peace would become a stranger to us.

What is purer than love? Yet it is very near the mud!

What is lovelier than love? Yet it is very near the abyss!

I do not think that we are ever more aware of the drama between heaven and earth, between purity and impurity, between dedication and selfishness, than in married love!

It is like walking in high mountains, on the crest of a glittering glacier: one slip is enough and you are in the abyss.

'Love gives way to hate.
Faithfulness turns into adultery.
Fatherhood turns into murder.
The angel turns into Satan.
And this is why we have to be on watch.'

St. Thomas himself said, 'If the radiance of chastity is praiseworthy within the walls of a convent, how much more praiseworthy it is amid the cares of the world.'

But what sustained vigilance has to be practised by married Christians!

I think that a very high degree of holiness is needed for chastity to be fully achieved in marriage, and I think young people are mistaken who suppose that marriage is the solution to everything. If premarital chastity is difficult, marital chastity is just as difficult, I might say even more so.

You have to be on your guard!

And sometimes, I may say, it is more urgent to watch than to pray. To avoid an occasion for sin is more difficult than saying the rosary.

'Be on guard even before marriage.
Above all in choosing whom you marry.'

A lad who seriously wants to achieve holiness in marriage should look for a girl who belongs to more or less the same social and cultural background as he does. This is most important. But it is even more important for him to be clear about what qualities he should look for in his future wife: generosity, willingness for sacrifice and a temperament sympathetic to the troubles of others.

If he doesn't feel sure about this, if he doesn't feel that his future mate will fulfil herself in charity, he should not begin the relationship, since no one can make a little church out of this sort of material: only a little sitting-room, or worse still a little chicken-house.

This is why I say that vigilance should immediately prompt the young man to speak clearly to his intended wife on two fundamental topics, both connected with the true Christian notion of marriage, this being possible only to someone who understands the value of sacrifice: the topic of children and the topic of loving our neighbour.

Between them, they should make a mutual promise, running more or less as follows:

1. We shall accept all the children which God's love sees fit to send us.

2. We shall not shut ourselves up in self-centred domesticity but shall go on, as far as circumstances permit, and even more than that, exercising our apostolate in those forms of social work which keep our individual family integrated in the human family at large.

And stay on your guard after making your choice.

There are some stern things that ought to be said to young engaged couples, but I can only bring myself to say these to avoid misleading them.

Vigilance is essential when love, going beyond heart and mind, invests the body too.

It becomes a fire.

It may seem hard, but to my young friends, to young people who want to crusade for holiness in marriage, I say this: Avoid, by offering these as a powerful sacrifice, any contacts producing physical excitement before marriage. I do not want young people to misunderstand me: love doesn't frighten me, but I am convinced that, in the times and moral climate in which we live, the law of heroic sacrifice is the only way to safeguard love and purity. If the sacrifice is made at the level of the senses, love will grow stronger at the level of the affections and at the level of conversation, and this will be all gain, since it begins the process of fusing your souls together: this being a fundamental preparation for the total fusion of two married Christians in accordance with God's command.

*   *   *

And be vigilant in marriage.

I have often pondered over St. Paul's awesome words to those about to get married, 'You will have the torment of the flesh.'

What does this mean? This is the background to the picture, depicting the titanic struggle between the flesh and the spirit, between pleasure and duty, between sensuality and the search for God.

And this is why I said that a perfect marriage is highest holiness.

And this is why I say that today's saints will be men and women who have succeeded in achieving the awe-inspiring synthesis of heaven and earth and have fully effected the mystical embodyment of Christianity in the world.

Poor men, yet having millions in the bank; obedient, yet being in charge; chaste, yet having beautiful and fascinating wives.

But at what cost of vigilance!

I have no hesitation in saying that grace alone can work the miracle and can work it only in men who are extremely vigilant.

Men who know how to say no.

Men who have been tempered in the fire.

Isn't it heroic to be sensitive in your initial intimate relationships and to approach your wife with a sensitivity appropriate to a living member of Christ?

Isn't it heroic to regulate the marital act by love and reason, and not by the senses?

Isn't it heroic to abstain from making love when your wife is not in good physical health, or is tired,

or is having her periods, or is pregnant, or immediately after childbirth?

Yes, heroism is God's sublime gift to the vigilant
souls who seek his help. Provided that after being
vigilant you know how to pray.

Pray! Pray! Pray!

If your home is a miniature church, prayer will be
its very breath.

Especially prayer for God's support:

'Dictate your ways to me, Yahweh,
    and teach me your paths.
Encourage me to walk true to you,
    since you are the God who will save me.
                                    (Ps 25:4–5)
How long am I to harbour doubts in my soul,
    thus generating sorrow in my heart?' (Ps 13:2)

'Come, said my heart, seek his face!
    O Yahweh, your face will I seek!
Do not turn your face away
    or angrily repulse me, but help me! (Ps 27:8–9)

'O God my God, I pine for you,
    how thirsty my soul is for you,
my body longing more for you
    than arid ground for drops of moisture!'
                                    (Ps 63:1)

Then the song of thanksgiving:

'I love you, Yahweh my Strength!

Yahweh is my Crag and my Eyrie!
With Death's breakers closing in on me,
    Belial's torrents going to swallow me,
Sheol's trip-wires every side of me
    and Death's traps lying ahead of me,
I called to Yahweh in my extremity
    and my cry for help reached his ears!'

                                    (Ps 18:1–6)

And victory will be ours!

8. More Intimate Than Ever

The husband speaks

Something may have been born . . .

'The familiar world is asleep, the rooms of our house
are silent, full of darkness. Beside the road, near the
woodland plants, stands our little house with our
great love locked up inside it. The leaves on the trees
droop like wings and the moonlight throws their
surfaces into relief. The house is asleep with the loving people who live in it. You too. Your face is as
pale as the moonlight and the hair framing your face
is as black as the night.

'We made love like two good-natured children,
like husband and wife of course: but as simply and
good-naturedly as though we were still two children
playing a game as artless and gentle as your eyes,
Maria.

'And now your eyes are asleep: I see them resting
behind two thin veils of eyelid. But earlier they
gazed at me, huge, dilated with love and wonder,
like a poet's eyes confronted with poetry. I was

beauty to you, just as you are beauty to my enamoured gaze. You, with your white limbs, with your body as thin as a wilting flower, yet firm and fertile as a plant loaded with fruit.

'We have been making love, Maria, and now perhaps, without our knowing, something has been born in the warmth within you as you lie sleeping here beside me – for I do not know and no one knows the great mystery of life.

'Little wife, without our knowing, perhaps something has been born and is already with us, near us, hidden in the mystery of your lovely body, asleep inside you.

'You and he sleep as one entity now, but tomorrow he will be looking us in the eye and asking to know the wherefore of this mysterious birth, and we shan't know what to tell him: except that we made love and loved the thought of him, the thought of the future him with our flesh, with our blood in his veins, and of all our mutual love transformed into a body and soul and living being.

'Perhaps tomorrow, little wife, we shall see him. But in the meanwhile, I see you. While everyone else is asleep and you too are asleep, I go on loving you and caressing you with my eyes.

'Sleep on, with your beautiful, virginal body, with your white breasts swollen with milk, and your mouth half-open as though you were still laughing at me.

'Wife, I plucked you like a flower, like a virgin flower unspotted: and this you still are. What you have lost has been transformed into gentleness, love, flesh and blood of new men born of you as wheat is born of the good earth.

'I took you when you were timid and reluctant, like a wild bird, and your eyes rolled and your hair flew wild in alarm as though love were a high wind.

'And now, you are as direct and loving as a tame dove and not afraid any more. Yet you have retained a modesty in giving yourself which always leaves something more to be taken and a new surprise whenever I touch you.

'You belong to me.

'Your body is mine and you yield it to me with modesty, so that I may love it with respect; at the same time, it is part of you – a warm little garment for your candid soul. And when I caress you, passion makes me love you even more as though you were the bark of, or your whole body the little leaf of, a tree growing underground, which I only glimpse by the light of your eyes. And this is what I love, even when loving your body; this is the life of the children which we shall see and which are now, as it were, hidden in our love and waiting to be born of us; this is God's glance alighting on us and kindling life beyond the warmth of our own lives.

'You kindle every kind of love in my heart; your spirit is the fire at which I warm myself. By its light, I see things more clearly, your body being the synthesis of all beauty, its perfect form embodying all forms.

'I look at you and think of what you are and of what you have given me; of your goodness which I absorb day by day, giving light to my life; and I think of the cradles which you have filled with children for me and of your mysterious nature with its daily promise of life.

'Your womb is a fruitful field, my daughter, my wife, and your breasts are innocent fruit for your pure children: your entire body is made for giving, just as your heart is made for loving. I take you and you give to me; you become my mother, you give me the riches of children who are indeed mine but are born exclusively of your suffering.

'My whole life consists in taking from you, and yours in smilingly giving yourself to me.

'How beautiful you are, dear wife. Perhaps something has been born, Maria, while you are sleeping there, innocently dreaming, and while I am watching you, thinking about love . . .!'

A wife speaks

A fire is lit

'There hasn't been much time since our wedding: hardly time for the new body, light as a flower of flesh growing from our united trunks, to take shape and blossom.

'Tonight, I need to remember and to talk, to talk at length, quietly while the last embers fade in the fireplace and the baby quietly goes to sleep on my lap.

'Come nearer, dear one, much closer, for the day is dark and it is so cold outside in the as yet untrampled snow.

'That morning it was so sunny and the sky between the clouds of one squall and the next seemed such a brilliant blue, as though washed and dripping with the rain suspended in the air and shimmering with light. The bells had woken us with a shock from what little sleep we had managed to get the previous night, and summoned us hurriedly to church. On the church steps, cleaned by last night's rain and wind, we eventually drew breath, our faces fresh and flushed from getting up so early and from the nervous haste with which we had got dressed. There wasn't a big crowd: just our tearful mothers, our pale fathers and a few friends silent and somewhat overcome.

'I was dressed entirely in white, in a flowing dress making me look taller: straight and slim as a church candle alight at the top with the warm blush of my face and the dull gold of my hair. And you were as dark as a sturdy oak-tree never to be blown down, though the wind might make it shake a little, as I was shaking that morning in that church ablaze with lights and overflowing with flowers.

'We knelt down together, the two of us, by ourselves in front of the altar; our shoulders were touching. When the priest put the question, we gave our assent more with our heads and breath than with our voices. We said yes quietly because our voices were shaking so much, but our hearts were beating like mad. I put my little hand quickly in your big warm one, and found my finger encircled with love's gleaming ring. On coming out, we said hallo to our friends and then went off on our own:

we went straight home. We didn't want to go away
on a honeymoon. We could go on our travels later,
but at that moment we wanted to take possession of
our home. We were impatient to be there on our
own, to look each other in the eye and, yes, to kiss
each other on the mouth – after gazing at each
other so long from afar! . . .

'Meanwhile the clouds had thickened again and
the threatening storm sent us hurrying for shelter.
And as we hurried along, we felt even happier at the
thought of a warm, solid house waiting to shelter us
from the rain and cold. I kept close to you to keep
warm and shelter from the wind behind your broad
shoulders. We reached the door as the first drops
began to fall. You wanted me to go in first because,
you said, the house belonged to me, the present
which you had given me – but I took your hand and
we went in together, since the house was and is ours
and belongs to both of us – which is why it is warm,
since neither of us is alone in it.

'We hastily shut the world and the rain outside
and the roaring of the hurricane died down as
though driven away from our sealed enclosure of
bright new glass.

'Around us everything was bright and neat, warm
and welcoming. We made a tour of the house, which
we had furnished and arranged together but which
had only now become ours. And we lingered a long
time in front of the fireplace. We had wanted an
open fire in our house, a coal and wood fire to warm
the hands and comfort the soul. It was already
alight. Our mothers had come earlier in stealth and

got it going with dry twigs from the wood, so as to give us a lively, crackling welcome.

'We sat down together by the fire and looked into each other's face, bright with the reflection of the fire, and we felt intensely happy to be on our own at last and near each other.

'The house was already stocked and ready to live in. The store-cupboard was full, there was bread in the bread-bin, a fire in the grate and by the fire was the cat. We hadn't wanted anyone else to be with us at this our first encounter, but the cat didn't disturb us. After purring for a while by the hearth, it climbed onto our knees and went to sleep. It seemed – like all our other nice simple things – a symbol of home and family. We stroked it and all at once it gave us a welcome as though it had always been living with us. It yawned, showing its little pink tongue between little white teeth, arched its back, straightened its tail and then rubbed its nose against our legs. Its fur was soft and warm and made me think of the flesh of a newborn child. New house, new fire, new cat. And soon there would be new babies too, I thought. Here we are. We want for nothing.

'We spent the whole day at home, looking at our surroundings and looking at each other. It was the first time we had been together for such a long time alone, and it was the first time we had ever felt so calm and secure, in the sign of the cross on our joined hands, henceforth uniting us with no more fear. Earlier, our love had been timid and fearful; we had been afraid of harming each other. Now however it could not do either of us any harm. What would have been a profanation before was now a holy and blessed consummation. Now we could look calmly at each other, ready for anything – a little nervously, perhaps, but certainly with no element of fear. And I allowed you to caress me, not as before when I was frightened; now I stayed docile and trusting under your hand and even ran my own hand gently over your head and buried it in your hair.

'Finally, evening brought our long day to a close. We watched the shadows slowly encroaching from the corners of the room and, when it got too dark and I began to feel nervous, at a stroke you flooded the room with a cheerful burst of light and we looked at each other to take new stock of each other by this new light and were happy that our little house should be throwing its light out into the darkness.

'Then, shutting the window so that no one should see us, trembling a little you put your arms round my shoulders and gently kissed me for the first time . . .

'Not many months have gone by, dear friend, hardly enough time since that evening for this little newborn body to have slowly taken shape in me.

'You know, I used to feel him growing inside me. I felt that he belonged to me and to you, to both of us, and to Someone higher than us; and it seemed to me that I was doing something wonderful, even if it is what all women do!

'And now I feel almost dismayed at having created

a miracle greater than myself and I can't understand how such a thing could have happened in the sweet mystery of my loving you and waiting.

'What a long time we have been talking, dear friend. And it is as dark now as it was that evening. But the fire burns as then and our faces warmly reflect its flames. And now there are three faces, not two.'

*   *   *

I have let others do the talking[1] and you know why.

These matters are difficult to discuss. You remember when I first talked to you about love and you gazed into the valley, skilfully trying to evade my eye?

Even so, you know how important these things are.

Alas for you if you haven't understood!

I think such things ought to be said on our knees, since they are the deepest part of God's stupendous and incomparable design. When I am walking by the sea or am in the fields or walking in the mountains, I feel heaven and earth vibrating under the mysterious bow performing the symphony of love and life, that wonderful image of a God who defined himself as being Love and Life.

Alas for you if you have not loved these things and have not appreciated them at their true value!

1 Jana Predieri, from the book *L'arcobaleno delle ore*, Il Giorno, Milan.

82   CARLO CARRETTO

Some time ago, when I was on a journey, I met a young man of twenty-five or thereabouts. During the day I had been conducting a conference on marriage and the young fellow asked if he might have a private word with me.

We went for a walk together in the evening.

The young man suddenly began talking about marriage and, to give me a clearer insight into his state of mind, showed me a letter written by his fiancée.

This is what it said: '. . . You know I love you and want to marry you, but I cannot conceal from you that I feel distaste at the thought that marriage entails physical relations. How I wish I could spend my life with you as a sister, cultivating our minds and affections, without having to put up with nasty things like that,' &c.

'What do you advise me to do?' the young man asked, 'for, you see, she is a very pious, unworldly girl.'

I must admit that what he said gave me something to think about. The letter did indeed show a natural restraint, but it also betrayed a misdirected basic training.[1]

---

1 Women's natural reservations about physical relations in marriage are prompted by a complex of psychological attitudes which have to be overcome by conscious self-giving in love.

Hence the need for thorough education on this delicate topic, if a conflict of conscience and a false conception of marriage is not to be the result.

Aren't I right then to feel worried about that
pious generation, now in their fifties, who thought of
marriage as something not perfectly spiritual and
brought the young up to feel distaste for marital
relations as something unworthy of the ascetical
life?

As though human beings didn't have bodies and
as though those bodies weren't God's wonderful
creation!

A pious generation, embarrassed at mentioning
the lavatory as something derogatory to the dignity
of man – and thanks to whom, my cousin at her convent school was taught that nuns never went to the
lavatory because they were nourished solely on
prayer!

You may laugh, but you ought to weep when you
think about the ill effects of such a false initial training for life.

Think of all the wives enduring torments of conscience until, unable to bear the tension any longer,
they finally brought themselves to speak – to be immediately enlightened by some sensible priest.

We ought, dear sister, to rebel against those
wicked people, we ought to rally the good ones and
have a great crusade to idealise the family and love.
For love was and is the central axis on which God
makes the world go round.

Marital relations? Are they degrading, are they
humanly unworthy if life is to be born into the world
as a result? Are they something less than spiritual if
a Benedict, a Francis, an Ignatius, a Thérèse of
Lisieux, were brought into the world by their

means? Are they less than lovely if as a result I now gaze at you here beside me?

No, God's design is entirely lovely and entirely holy. To obey his will confers sweetest peace and inner joy, and marital relations are part of his will.

To young people preparing for marriage, who have not yet discovered all the reasons for spiritually idealising their vocation and who are particularly worried about sacrificing their virginity (something truly divine!) as their most jealously guarded and precious possession, I like to repeat this bold thought: Have you ever considered what joy God felt when he was creating the world? How he exulted in seeing orderly creation emerging from chaos and in giving body and form to things under the sway of his will? Right, you too will experience a pale reflection of that joy when in an ecstasy of love, in intimate relations with your wife, you draw the face, the body of your son out of the chaos of non-existence.

Besides, isn't everything connected with motherhood wonderful?

Try and think of your own mother. You will see that everything becomes pure.

I remember the day when I really grasped this.

One of my best friends rang me up. 'Carlo, I'm scared. Tonight my wife is going to have a baby. The doctor is worried about her; so are we all. Would you do me a favour? Would you come and spend the night with us?'

I agreed to go. That evening I climbed the hill in

Turin to the clinic where my friend's wife had been taken.

What a night! I can still hear the screams of pain coming from the delivery-room, and echoing un-muffled off the shining tiles of the corridor where I was waiting.

Rosary in hand, I paced back and forth in the dark. Every so often my friend would come out, pale and distracted. Clutching my hand, he would say, 'Pray, pray for her to be alright!'

The screams of pain had in no way diminished and for the first time I had an insight into the drama of all women struggling to give life to their children.

Suddenly the surgeon came out carrying a bundle of flesh, pink and crying. 'She's safe!' my friend exclaimed, throwing his arms round me.

Then came the dawn. A dawn quiet and without a breath of breeze, as though not to disturb the woman who had let herself be opened like a seed-pod so that the earth would not become a lifeless desert.

I walked back down the hill into the sleeping city.

The streetlights were still on in the streets.

When I got home, I went up to my mother's room. At once, she sat up in bed and said, 'How did she get on?'

Poor mother: from the tone of voice in which she asked the question, I grasped what I had never grasped till then: what I had cost her, how much I had cost her!

Poor mother!

And I kissed her as I had never kissed her before!

9. Being a Father

My flesh is athirst for children.
My heart is athirst for children.
My soul is athirst for children.
And you, being part of me, are athirst for them too.

Were it not so, we should both be sick, as those contemporaries of ours are infinitely so who have deadened that thirst at the putrid fountains of egoism.

The thirst for children is nature, the thirst for children is charity, the thirst for children is art, beauty, joy, life: in a word it is man's sharing in the loving, insatiable will exerted by God in creating the universe.

Anyone who doesn't feel this thirst has not only abdicated from being a son of God, but also from being a son of Man.

Today the lack of this thirst is particularly grave, not only as manifested by wicked people, but by so-called good ones too.

To the insensibility of modern man, I prefer the humanity of the Ancients.

Listen to these marvellous pages from the Bible:

In the land of Haran lived a man called Abram the Obedient. The Lord said to Abram: Leave your native land and your ancestral home and go to the country which I shall indicate.

Abram left his native land forthwith, for the land of Canaan as the Lord instructed.

He became a shepherd and God's blessing was with him.

Oceans of wool undulated round his shepherd's legs, and horses and camels made him one of the richest men in those parts.

His tents were soft with carpets and his coffers crammed with money, but this was not the wealth that a son would have been. His stockyard was bursting with life, but there was no baby's cry to make Abram happy.

He found the loneliness unbearable and each time his flocks gave birth making him richer than ever, he felt sadder than ever too.

'Give me a son,' was his constant prayer to Heaven.

But the years went by, old age drew on and the prayer never altered:

'Give me a son, O Lord!'

One day, God led him out into open country and said, 'Look up at the sky and count the stars if you can. Just so,' he added, 'shall be your offspring.'

It seemed like a cruel joke on God's part, but Abram believed and this was reckoned to him as righteousness.

To him was born Isaac, 'the son of smiling', who

grew up like a lamb, so white and tender was he.

His old father watched him sleeping on the sheepskins in his tent and skipping through the contented flocks with his hair flying in the wind.

Abram's thirst is all men's thirst; Abram's joy is all men's joy.

The gift of fatherhood is one of God's greatest favours to mankind, a share in his own joy in being a father.

I remember the misery among the rich and selfish people of Northern Italy, where they used regularly to murder unborn children with a total indifference; where they practised birth-control with the dropper of selfishness and the thermometer of lack of faith in God.

And I also remember the joy among the very poor people of Sardinia, rich in children and in love.

I shall never forget seeing a roadman, the father of eleven, sitting beside the mainroad and weeping like a child because his wife had had a miscarriage when he was looking forward to seeing the little face of his twelfth.

I saw a vast wealth in those manly tears, as I was later to see limitless poverty in the words of a woman who told my mother that she had taken good care not to bring any brats of her own into the world.

Today when I run across similar situations, I feel sad and take my yardstick of true civilisation not from shiny tiled bathrooms or table manners but from people's attitudes to the fundamentals of life.

If those bathrooms could speak, they would

chronicle the unheard cries of children never born, thanks to the selfishness of the so-called 'civilised'.

And for sure, if they are civilised, I prefer barbarians.

Aren't I right, my dearest?

But thank God a revolt is coming; a generation of young married and engaged couples steps forward with a burning desire to build the family as God conceived it. What a lot of them I know! What poems these young people write!

Listen to this letter written to me by Cesare Crespi who is one of them. In it he relates his feelings on the night when he became a father.

Dear Carlo,

I am writing to you from my flat. It is one o'clock in the morning. My wife is sleeping peacefully in the next room; she still bears the marks of great pain on her face. Within reach beside her is the wicker basket with our baby daughter sound asleep in it, her little fists stuck into her eyes, full up after the last breast-feed of the night.

If I close my eyes, I seem to go back in time and relive, minute by minute, the hours preceeding Maria's birth.

We had prayed so much in those previous weeks and months. We hadn't talked very much. Every time I looked at my wife's swollen belly or saw her sitting down in the posture typical of pregnant women, with her hands crossed lovingly over her belly, I felt immensely happy. She would intercept my glance and smile back. And would joke about the creature making her mother suffer before being born; we made happy threats against the creature already dominating our conversation. I would never have believed that I could have felt such joy over a little being which at that point had not even come into the world.

When, after examining my wife, the midwife told us that the child would be born in two or three hours' time, I felt as though my heart had stopped, and said, 'Are you sure you're right?' And instantly invoked the Motherhood of the Blessed Virgin.

I became acutely agitated. I paced up and down the room, shuttling back and forth between dining-room and bedroom. Every now and then I would take my wife's hand as she lay deserted on the edge of the bed, and kiss it hard as though to help her. Then I would start pacing up and down again. A thousand thoughts passed through my head: Is she in any danger? Will everything be alright? Will the child have something wrong with it? Mother of Heaven . . . think of us!

Then I tried saying, '*Non mea voluntas sed tua . . .*' but found it very hard to do so.

I was clutching my rosary, repeating the prayers and trying to prepare my soul for God's will, whatever that might be: but how hard that was!

Time went slowly by – 4.30, 5.00, 5.30, 5.45. I could hear my wife groaning in the titanic effort of bringing the baby into the world, and the midwife giving orders and the neighbours who were helping giving encouragement.

It was now the last five minutes before the child

was born. Once again God was showing his greatness by calling human beings to take part in his work of creation.

The house was drowned in shrieks of pain – and yet it was an anthem of praise.

I heard the bells of the parish church ring out for early Mass. I stopped pacing up and down and knelt in prayer, facing the statue of the Sacred Heart. My two sisters, who were now awake, were praying beside me.

I could hear the slow striking of the clock on the sideboard and the exhausted groans of my dear wife.

Then I heard a loud scream. Then a few seconds of silence. Then the midwife's cheerful voice exclaiming, 'It's a girl!'

And soon after that, the baby's first cry.

We jumped to our feet and my sisters threw their arms round me in floods of tears. And I could feel scalding tears of joy coursing down my own face: of immense, hitherto unimaginable joy and at the same time a sense of peace filling my heart.

I rushed into the bedroom and there I saw the loveliest baby-girl in the world, with a milky complexion, waving her tiny arms.

Why had I been told that babies are ugly, red and dirty when they are born? It wasn't true, or I couldn't see for looking!

I threw myself on my knees beside the bed and embraced my wife who was smiling at me through her tears.

We recited the Magnificat together, but more tears than words came out.

I bent over the baby, looking at her from close up. How graceful and fragile her little limbs were! My soul sang at the sight.

Then the baby began gently crying and I felt a vague sense of fear.

No, there was no reason for us to be afraid. God would not abandon people who had just completed the courageous act of calling a human being into life. The whole Church ought to give thanks for our having contributed to making her grow: the Mystical Body of Christ. Perhaps by means of us, she would be the richer for a saint!

I ran off to tell my brother-in-law who lived nearby.

I slipped into church in time to take Holy Communion.

What a wonderful communion that was!

When I got home I found the baby washed, dressed and already asleep at her mother's side, where my wife smilingly displayed her.

Doesn't that strike you as beautiful?[1]

Doesn't it sound like a psalm, fit to be sung in church?

1 Marriage may seem to be presented in over-idealised terms in this passage, especially when we reflect on the matter-of-fact maturity of people these days and on the unconstructive scepticism that goes with it. The author, however, adopted this treatment intentionally, thinking of the need, where young people are concerned, to re-awaken love and faith in their ideals, not, however, concealing the fact that this is to be achieved only by following the arduous path of duty.

So let us hear what a real psalm has to say about
the grandeurs of fatherhood and motherhood:

'If Yahweh does not build the palace,
    in vain the builders toil at it;
if Yahweh does not guard the city,
    in vain the guards keep watch.

'Failure to you who get up early
    and put off going to bed,
depending on idols for your food!
    The Reliable One makes his beloved prosper!

'Sons too are a bounty from Yahweh,
    progeny being his reward.
Like arrows in a warrior's hand
    are the sons you father in your youth.

'How blest the man who has filled his quiver
    with arrows of this sort!
Undaunted, from the city gate
    he will repulse his foes.' (Ps 127)

These are the words of revelation: hence the
truth.
    Isn't it a fine image: the sons compared to arrows
in a warrior's hand?
    May God grant a full quiver!

10. They Will Always Need Us

When children are in their mother's womb, their mother is all they need.

Her warm, loving womb is their table, their school and their playground. In it they breathe life, they take on their first features, they begin to know laughter and sorrow – almost invariably their mother's laughter and sorrow.

In it they complete the first and most important stage of their education.

Then, as though impatiently wanting a better view of things, they came forth into the light. It is as though the mother's womb had expanded, now that they are bigger, and the whole house has become a womb, in which they breathe, eat, play, in a word, live. Then to the mother is added the father, then all the other people: relations, the open window, the yard, voices, songs, all contribute to this second phase of education.

Later there is the addition of street, church, school, sky, earth, factors sometimes conscious, sometimes not, in the awesome and fundamental drama called 'bringing up children'.

But although all these things contribute, although all have something to add, it is nonetheless certain that the major responsibility, that the greater burden, that the major anxiety will always lie with the father and mother.

These the children will always need, even after the parents are dead – for such is God's will.

To educate means 'to lead', but it is important to know 'where to lead'. The Christian does know and thus has a great advantage over others who do not.

There are highly intelligent and cultivated people who do not know which way to go and their educational efforts lack one very simple thing: an aim. These, Jesus would still say, are the blind leading the blind.

Educating, that is to say leading, a boy is no easy thing. The ancients used to talk of education in terms of sculpture, or of the art of those who wrote in wax. Others preferred to compare it with farming. In all these comparisons there is an element of truth, but they are not completely apt since the stone is inanimate, whereas the boy can move; the wax is static, but the boy is free; the plant is alive, but has no inner life.

Our contemporaries talk about natural relationships, about loving relationships, and Christians about relationships in charity. And there is much good in this too. If nothing else, one indisputable truth emerges: you cannot do without the educator.

A boy left to himself will live like a savage, like a wild plant, like a disordered household.

And this is because nature itself is diseased.

And if nature is diseased, the doctor is needed.

The educator is the doctor.

I prefer to call the teacher a doctor: like Jesus, whom I often invoke in my prayers as the sweet doctor of my soul.

Millions of books could be written on how children ought to be brought up. Here I shall confine myself to four main headings, which young parents can elaborate for themselves:

Training in humility.

Training in purity.

Training in piety.

Training in the apostolate.

Training in humility

I put this first because today it is the most neglected. I have often found Christian parents who were completely unacquainted with this truth; you could say, they did not even know where to begin.

Scene: the evening. We are in a young couple's home. He is reading the paper, she is getting supper ready. The toddler is playing. Peace.

The waters stir. The toddler begins chasing the cat, then gets hold of a chair and drags it into the kitchen. He aims a kick at his toy horse which ends up in the bucket. He is cross.

He goes to the table and reaches up to grab a plate. Father happens to notice, stops reading and rescues the plate. He goes on with his reading without a word. The little one, gently pushed away, returns to the assault; at home he is the boss. The plate is grabbed again but this time is saved by Mummy's unexpected intervention.

You little monkey, what are you doing with that plate? —with a pat, she sends the little ruffian on his way.

But the game is amusing, and well knowing how weak his parents are, the tiny tot returns to the attack. This time he really gets the plate and rushes round the house with his booty. Father stops reading and rather crossly goes to catch the child, whereupon Mummy says, 'Don't hurt him. He only wants to play. I understand.'

Carefully and smilingly she whisks the plate out of his hands, while their young hopeful's fertile brain thinks up a new plan of campaign. At the fourth attack the plate falls on the floor and the useless expostulations of the two cowards emphasise the tyrant's victory. He sheds a few crocodile tears and completes his triumph by wheedling a teaspoonful of sugar and these admirable words from Mummy: 'Naughty Daddy, to frighten you like that! Let's give Daddy whack-whacks! Now be good, &c.' And that's the end of that peaceful evening.

That's how 80% go on today.

And when you think that all that was needed to stop these antics was a little strength and decisiveness at the outset!

The child might have cried perhaps, but at least over something worth crying about: a sharp slap.

He ought to have been made to stand in the corner and not been spoken to until he could see that he was beaten. And then would have come out to be the light and joy of his Mummy and Daddy, whose authority he would have henceforth respected.

Lack of authority in the modern family is probably its most widely diffused malady. And the evil is no longer confined, as it used to be, to middle-class families but is now attacking the industrial working-classes and even the country people too.

These people will have to open their Bibles again and read these apposite maxims:

'A man who loves his son will beat him frequently so that in after years the son may be his comfort.

'A man who is strict with his son will reap the benefit,
    and be able to boast of him to his acquaintances.

'A man who coddles his son will bandage his wounds
    and his heart will jump into his mouth at every shout.

'A horse un-broken turns out stubborn
and a son left to himself turns into a hooligan.

'Do not leave him at liberty when he is young
and do not turn a blind eye to his caprices.

'Bend his neck while he is young

or he will grow stubborn and disobedient.'

(Si 30:1—12)

This is God speaking, who does not deceive us.

I earnestly implore young parents: be strict. Don't be frightened of your children's tears – they are a good diet.

Training in humility is founded on respect for authority. The very young ought to be trained to respect authority. The child should not have the last word, and both parents should be in agreement on this. Woe to them if they contradict each other in front of their children, woe to them if they give way! [1]

It is also a mistake to praise children too easily. A word of praise after a battle won, after a good deed, after a dull job finished, does good, praise being like a drop of oil in the engine; but to flood a child with praise is an act of weakness. Training in humility

---

1 Exercising your authority and being forceful about it does not mean that you are lacking in love. What it does mean is establishing a harmonious and peaceful relationship with your children, based on respect for age – a relationship which children seek and love, whatever it costs them. A child loves a strongminded father who knows what he wants, since he then feels secure and in good hands.

In every case, when you exert your authority – usually a little is enough, if you act decisively – you ought to bear these few simple principles in mind:

a) a scolding, let alone a slap, should never be given in a fit of temper;

b) the scolding should be 'rational' and something which the child can understand;

c) you must make the severity of your action proportionate to the seriousness of the misdeed;

d) you must be as consistent as possible, *always*, regardless of how you feel.

entails the parents' not displaying too much outward attention to their children. They ought to give the impression of ignoring many of their actions and of setting no store by their potential abilities. When there are other people in the house, they should take even less notice of them, keeping them at a distance and not letting them talk all the time. Children should feel that they are not important, that they count for little, that they are the last comers and ought to be quiet and unobtrusive.

Quite the reverse of what happens in some middle-class households, where one has hardly got inside the door before Mummy and Daddy are vying with each other to push the child forward for attention: a school of vanity and pride, indeed! 'Come along, darling! Recite your nice poem for Uncle Carlo!'

And the child, aware of being the apple of their eyes, bridles artfully, takes an exasperatingly long time in being cajoled and still gets its own way in the end!

Training in purity

Here again, a few simple words where a whole volume might be devoted to the subject.

Training in purity is for the most part done by example, in most households without being mentioned at all. The children of the house absorb the equilibrium, restraint, modesty and purity of their parents. Purity is not a gnarled old tree, but a flower born of wholesome soil. If the ground isn't wholesome, the flower will not be born. It is useless to over-emphasise purity in an obsessive sense. It will not subsist in the soul if other things are lacking, especially piety. I repeat: purity is a flower born in ground which isn't swampy. If it is a swamp, where people don't pray, where they don't believe in God, where they don't know the meaning of sacrifice, cultivating it is labour lost.

I was once invited to speak about purity in a prison. I had intended to deliver very lofty spiritual truths on this important virtue. After the opening prayer, however, I admit that, faced with that crowd in their distinctive prison garb, I thought my material unsuitable and began to talk about the existence of God. I realised that there was no point in talking about the fruit before talking about the tree. How can anyone be pure who doesn't believe in God? How can anyone not aware of God's presence possibly withstand temptation?

Purity in children is achieved by practising all the other virtues and above all that of piety.

At a given moment, parents find themselves confronted with the important duty of explaining the facts of life to their children. And here I should like to offer a word of advice.

I have already said that the majority of families find it easier to adopt the tactics of silence and avoid any mention of these matters. If a child asks a question, the mother more or less skilfully evades it, invents a fib or tells it to be quiet.

Nothing is more damaging that tactics of this sort.

I think the Devil must have prompted good Christian people to adopt them, to facilitate a massacre of the innocents. If the mother will not give an answer, the child will save the question up for another occasion. Naturally, it won't be his parents whom he asks next time; instead he will find an opportunity for asking one of his school-friends, with a vague sense of touching on a forbidden subject. The first word of life's sublime poem will be learnt from some snotty-nosed kid whose leers will give the immediate impression that love is sin.

The child will go on attending school, either on his own or in a gang, regularly or intermittently acquiring such a mass of misinformation as may perhaps poison his whole youth.

And the family meanwhile pursues its sublime strategy of saying nothing.

No, no, no! This won't do, since it falls short of the educators' real duty, for which the parents are nothing if not responsible. And how can the matter be passed over in silence, when it is the axis of the universe, round which all human life revolves? Because we are afraid to tackle it? And yet parents expect their children to confide in them! How can you expect them to confide in you if you shut the door on this most vital of questions? If you put them off with lies? Or if you merely smile, deluding yourself that the child is far too young to be able to understand?

No, take your child in your arms and explain. Don't be afraid. Maria Purissima will bring suitable words and innocuous illustrations to your lips, rather than let your child's soul be troubled.

God's power will give you the necessary grace to discharge your task, to enlighten, to do good. And your child will love you the better, the better he understands.

And when he knows that it isn't true that he was found under a cabbage leaf but that you, dear mother, have carried him inside you for nine months, close to your heart, and that he blossomed out of you like a flower, he will love you all the more.

And when he knows that you suffered to give him life, as every seed must suffer to bear a sprout, he will kiss you even harder.

Don't be afraid. Speak! I am not going to teach you what to say. God himself will teach you that. He will not let you take the wrong road.

And then there is the Church, who is a mother like you, more of a mother than you. Ask what she does, consult your spiritual director and then speak!

See how the prayer begins: 'Hail Mary, full of grace, for the Lord is with you. Blessed art thou among women and blessed the fruit of your womb, Jesus!'

Speak about Mary's womb, about that sublime church which once housed Christ, and so proceed.

There is no need to go into details and it is better not to do so. Above all, it is better to say nothing about the physiology of the sex-act, better not to go into anatomical explanations. A veil should be left over all this. Nature will do the instructing in due course and the soul will not be troubled.

But everything else, yes – everything concerning

the family, concerning love, concerning children. Above all, make him understand what love is for, what marriage is for, the rightness and sublimity of love and the moral grandeur of the family.

Don't you agree?

Training in piety

This is the hardest and most important of all. It means bringing the child into contact with God. It means training him to talk to God and to be aware of God.

Humanly speaking, this would be impossible to do, if God didn't come to our help. On our own, none of us could even say 'A', and could certainly never have acquired the notion that God is called 'Abba', which is to say, Father.

But here God himself will intervene, drawing the soul to himself and sending his divine Spirit to lead the child to a knowledge of the Eternal.

Piety doesn't only mean the inner life.

Yet the whole thing may be briefly and completely put like this:

'God loves me and for love of me sacrificed his son, Jesus.'

It is thus enough if you talk about Jesus.

Jesus is the essence of piety. He is piety itself.

We must teach our children who Jesus is.

Jesus himself will do the rest.

If I had anything else to add, I should say: Try to explain what the world was like without Jesus — darkness, death, despair, helplessness.

Then the heavens opened and the Son of God took flesh and became our brother.

He became part of our family, one of us, and taught us how we ought to behave (the Gospel) and, to give us the strength to carry out what he taught, gave us an all-powerful medicine: his Blood, his Flesh.

With food like this, the climb to heaven became possible even for the most worn-out, even for the feeblest.

Once I have managed to make Jesus known to my children, I shall have nothing more to fear. They will look for him for themselves for the rest of their lives, in the Eucharist and the Gospel.

And all the rest will come in due course!

Training in the apostolate

This is the largest revolution which has to be made in the educational field.

Christianity as practised by all-too-many middle-class people has been reduced to a lifeless, bite-less system of observances.

Many, many families who boast of being Christian, train their children to 'go to church'. As long as this particular duty is discharged, the vaguest notions suffice for everything else.

For these people, being a Christian means 'going to Mass', not 'living the pulsating life of Christ'; being good means 'performing your Easter duty', not 'proclaiming the Kingdom of the Father'.

This disease, moreover, is very wide spread and has even extended its lethal influence into many so-called Christian boarding-schools. In such places, Christianity is no stronger, no more vigorous, than elsewhere. It is only a formality.

It is reduced to a few services and a few petty practices. The apostolate is non-existent, not mentioned, being thought of as the sole concern of the cloth.

If these so-called teachers only knew: to deprive Christianity of its driving force, of the impulse to win others for Christ, is in fact to sterilise it, to make it unappealing to the young and to turn it into a museum exhibit!

The apostolate is the life-blood of Christianity.

And we must devote ourselves to it.

In training our children, we must never divorce thought from deed, or faith from works.

When we teach our children about Jesus, that same day they should feel the need to pass on what we have told them to others.

When we teach them about the poor and how Christ lives in them, that same day we should take them by the hand and go and visit the poor in the garrets of great houses or in the hovels of the countryside.

When I tell my son that communism is a heresy seducing working-folk with the promise of improved working conditions to make them into slaves of the state, that same day he ought to be fired with that same zeal for truth as I am, and hold a meeting of his own age-group. And I shall not reproach myself if I see him coming home with grazed knuckles and a bloody nose.

Christianity is action, not falling asleep; is life, not death; is heat, not frost.

This is the kind of family I dream of: a little citadel of heroic Christians, an apostolic community where every member acts, works, suffers for the one great truth and for the one great and true love: the Kingdom of God.

That is what I should like, and then my family would never lack a soul, a cause or a school!

Very different from the sluggish, soft, gutless, middle-class-Christian family, whose home is like a hotel, merely used for eating and sleeping, where no spiritual conversation flourishes, where all serious matters are tangential, where people die of boredom and where their ruling concern is whether their children pass their Eleven Plus and O-Levels.

No, we must build an apostolic family: where people talk about God and his Kingdom, where the urge to win souls for Christ is vigorous and active, and where Christ's great commandment is put into practice: 'Seek first the Kingdom of God and his righteousness, and everything else will be added to you.'

A family which, on moving to a new district, regards it as a new mission-field.

In a word, a family which is the Church in miniature, an image of the greater Church, I mean the parish, and of that huge Church, Christendom itself.

11. The Loveliest of Secrets

Shall we go for a walk in the dark, dearest?

Feel how still and warm the air is! There won't be any dew tonight and we can sit on that tree-trunk by the spring at the edge of the meadow.

I want to enjoy the words reaching us from the stars, to enjoy what the water has to say and the breathing of the natural things around me, the quiet, peaceful breathing of the creation resting under the watchful eye of God.

Lean your head against my shoulder.

Your touch makes me all the more vividly aware of the presence of Infinite Love, more warmly aware of the caress of the Invisible Presence enfolding us in his love.

Tonight I want to tell you my life's most treasured secret, something I have rarely shared, something dearer to me day by day.

This is it: I believe in God's love.

I believe in his smile. I feel his presence, prompting me, pleading with me, speaking to me. I can feel him loving me.

From the moment I discovered this to be true, I

have been rid of fear. Pain and death have changed their aspect too.

I do not think of God as mysterious, distant, passive, motionless, way beyond the stars, never touched by, never intervening in, my life's affairs. I think of and believe in God as living, present, loving, intervening, never foresaking me for a second, watching over me and interested in me, as father, brother, friend, no, I go even further: as husband.

You see, my very love for you and yours for me are images of his love. Thinking of you, I find it easier to think of him; experiencing your love, which is the highest and most absolute of loves, I find a more perfect figure of his love.

He loves me!

What are the logical consequences to be deduced from this?

To grasp them, I have only to think of you. What would I not do for you? And you, what wouldn't you do for me? How could I not be aware of you, how could I not want what's best for you? How could you forget me? How could I not help you? If you were to call, would I not reply?

How human loneliness vanishes, bathed in divine love! Everything grows full, takes colour, comes alive, feels sweeter.

I fear nothing now that I have grasped the truth: He is with me. There is no more emptiness, since he fills all. There is no real suffering, no real death, since he loves me and fills me with his life to overflowing.

And what bliss to lie back in his almighty arms!

You understand, when this truth is yours, that the world and life look different. Anxiety? Terror? Worries? Loneliness? Empty words. Nothing, nothing alarms any more.

Listen to the sweet words of Scripture:

'Yahweh is my shepherd –
  what more can I want!
In green fields will he make me rest,
  by quiet waters guide me
  there to refresh my soul –
into rich pastures lead me
  as befits his name.

'Even were I to walk
  in the most utter darkness,
I should not fear the Evil One
  since you are with me.' (Ps 23:1–4)

Believing this is my most precious secret, and I want it to be your most precious secret too.

This is the quintessence of all piety, the soul of every prayer, the inner sweetness of all religious experience.

And this is the basic battle to be fought throughout our lives.

Even though we shall not be spared ordeals, and sometimes God will seem to turn away and hide and not hear us when we call.

But that is the very time when we need to believe more firmly.

When all is going well and we have plenty of share-certificates in the strongroom at the bank and the store-cupboard is overflowing and our job is assured with a decent pension to follow, it is easy enough to pay tribute to God's providence.

But when the house is falling down and unemployment is knocking at the door, when enemies gang up and our wallet is empty and the children are clamouring for food, oh then faith may begin to wobble under the blows of hardship and our alleged trust in God blow away like dust in a storm.

Yet this is the very moment when our faith and trust should bind us most closely to him for he wills to reveal himself to us in all love's guises: as father, friend, brother and indeed as husband. Believing in him in spite of everything and everyone, believing in him when hope has humanly vanished and when danger makes us shudder to the core.

For even pagans can believe in providence when nothing is amiss, when a thousand have to meet a hundred foes, when there are £30,000 available for a project which will cost only £5,000 at most.

But the Holy Books give very different examples of trust in the Most High.

Three lads at the court of an idolatrous king find themselves in the inescapable dilemma of having to offend God by worshipping a statue, or of having to offend Nebuchadnezzar by refusing to knuckle under. Life or death: the choice is yours!

They choose death and, armed only with faith in God, enter the flames, saying:

'The God whom we adore is able to save us from

the burning fiery furnace and from your power, O
king' (Dn 3:17).

And the miracle occurs: the flames part and
Ananiah, Azariah and Mishael haven't a single hair
singed between them.

There was once a young married woman in a garden in the East. Two old men, spying on her with
lustful eyes, made her this proposition: Either you
submit to us or we denounce you to the people as an
adulteress and say that we saw you sinning with a
young man.

The only choice that poor Susanna has is between
sinning and living, or resisting and dying.

'I prefer to fall innocent into your power than to
sin in the eyes of the Lord,' she replies strong-
mindedly, putting her trust entirely in God (Dn
13:23).

Death is a certainty, the evidence of the two old
men hangs together: how can God intervene?

But intervene he will.

Inspired by God, Daniel steps forward. He stops
the procession of people escorting Susanna to stone
her to death.

'Who accuses this innocent woman? Come here,
you two old men, your sins have found you out and
now you will pay the price of your wickedness.'

The two old men, having been separated, now
had to reply to Daniel's questioning.

Said the prophet to one, 'Tell me, oh you who
have grown old in wickedness, where you saw
Susanna doing wrong?'

'Under the mastic tree,' he replied.

'That barefaced lie will recoil on your own head.'
Next came the other old man.

'Spawn of Canaan and not of Judah, beauty has seduced you but Susanna will not suffer for your iniquity. Tell me, if you saw her sinning, under which tree was she doing it?'

'Under the holm-oak,' the old man replied.

'This too is a barefaced lie which will recoil on your head, for the Angel of the Lord is waiting, sword in hand, to cut you in half and put you both to death' (Dn 13: 46–59, paraphrase).

The conflict of evidence saved the chaste woman and procured the death sentence for her traducers.

Belief in God! Belief in him right to the end: what a dramatic choice is ours!

This is the highest expression of all religious faith; this is the quintessence of mysticism.

'Should you pass through the sea, I shall be with you;
    or through rivers, they will not swallow you up.
Should you walk through fire, you will not be scorched;
    through flame, it will not burn you.
For I am Yahweh your God,
    the Holy One of Israel, your Saviour.'

(Is 43:2–3)

Feeling these words to be addressed to us and living them in their most literal sense, means 'believing in God'.

How changed our lives would be! Fears, worries,

the future, pain, death? All these would lose their
negative aspect, and like children we should feel
ourselves being lulled in the arms of the most loving
of mothers.

If you trust in God . . .
'You will go on your way in all safety,
    your feet will not stumble.
When you go to sleep you need not be afraid,
    when you lie down, sweet will be your slumber.
Have no fear of sudden terror
    nor of assault by wicked men,
since Yahweh will be your guarantor,
    he will keep your steps from the snare.'

(Pr 3:23–26)

Could there be any greater joy than to live by the
light of this? Could any peace be more complete?
Believing in God, believing in his omnipotence, in
his omniscience and above all in his love!

Yet, if God is what he is, things ought to be like
this. Everything should be caught up in a universal
harmony in which not a blade of grass can escape
his wisdom and power.

Everything should be an expression of the Infinite
Love which has created the actual and potential
universe, has redeemed it with an indescribable
abyss of loving kindness, and which one day will
achieve its ends in infinite ability and power.

Can anything really bad happen to anyone who
puts his trust in this almighty King of Love?

What nonsense that would be!

Some people may object: But illness, death,

poverty, tears are equally the heritage of those who trust in God and pray to him!

Quite true!

But is our crying 'really something bad' when united to the tears of Jesus the Redeemer? Doesn't it become a diadem of pearls for life eternal?

But is death 'really something bad' when it is the '*porta coeli*', when it is immolation in union with Christ's immolation?

Anyhow, is the real life here, or there?

How diseased with earthliness our generation is, how middle-class our Christianity, staking all on the contingent and setting nothing by the eternal!

And again: the fact of death reveals the colossal fraudulence of life, whereas we go on incurably deceiving ourselves and hoping for our paradise on earth.

No, that is not God's plan and, not being God's plan, ought not to be man's plan either. We must acquire a more mature, more realistic vision.

And that vision is precisely faith in him: total, complete, joyous.

And then we shall know what peace really means.

Yes, at the dawn of a stormy day, or in the evening coming home from work, or on the battlefield before the attack, or facing the gloomy future with tears in our eyes, we shall slowly, slowly recite the verses of the psalm:

'Who sits enthroned in the shelter of the Most High,

who passes the night in the shadow of Shaddai,
well may he say, 'Yahweh, my refuge, my eyrie,
    my God, in whom I put my trust!'

'Yes, he will free you from the snare,
    will protect you from whatever is poisonous,
he will cover you with his pinions
    and under his wings you will find refuge:
    his arm will be shield and protector.

'You need not fear marauders of the night
    or the flying arrow of the day,
the plague that prowls in the dark
    or the scourge that stalks at high noon.'

(Ps 91:1–6)

And our confidence will return.

*   *   *

And this is true, especially on the threshold of
marriage.

Look, one of the theme-songs I hear all too often,
even from Christians, is this: Children, certainly . . .
but who's going to pay for their upbringing?

Married people's lives are bedevilled with the
blackest worries and their relationships are
poisoned by the most pagan considerations
imaginable.

As I see it, these people haven't discovered life's
most precious secret, the secret which gives peace,
tranquillity, joy, even in the most terrifying storms.

I once heard a teacher, who called himself a Christian, giving a talk to young people on the eve of marriage. He loaded his lecture with a whole series of worries, he listed so many matrimonial dangers, with the pious intention of inculcating prudence, that by the time he had finished he had turned the most impressive and sublime of God's designs into a complicated and virtually insoluble problem of dual co-habitation.

How many children should they have? And when are the infertile periods? And what is the rule here, and what is the rule there? In a word, he seemed more like a juggler using morality – this vaunted morality of the middle-classes – to outwit the omnipotence of God.

No, that is not the way to increase people's love for God, or to give peace to their souls, or to put the fire of God's loving presence into their hearts!

I put the whole thing the other way round and boldly say: God loves me and in this truth all problems are resolved.

How complicated human beings are! And how they reduce everything to problems, not realising that if everything is a problem, one thing at least is not one: love.

And if God loves me, for me there are no more substantial problems, except the one of how to stay near him. And if God loves me and knows me (as he does), he will know how much weight to lay on my poor shoulders. And if God loves you and knows you (as he does, since he is omniscient and omnipotent), he will know exactly how many children to give you for your love, your womb, your blood, your strength to bear. Not one more, and not one less.

Don't you think this is the right sort of attitude for someone who believes in God?

Our trust in him should be total, deep in our very bones.

We shall want for nothing. By miracle after miracle, he will intervene in answer to our faith. Each child that arrives will bring his own little hamper with him; our own abilities are not what are going to solve the problem of how to provide for him — God's infinite love will do that.

This is not to say that things will be comfortable or easy. This is not to say that all our sons will become lawyers and engineers. This is not to say that they will be dressed in soft raiment. But it is to say that they won't die before fulfilling their mission, it is to say that they won't lack for a crust, that their vocation will open up before them, that peace and joy will ever be in their hearts, because God is with them.

How I should like to pass this faith on to every young married couple! How much the happier they would be! How the shadow of doubt would be lifted from their hearts! How much more their love-making would mean to them! How much braver, gayer, serener they would be!

Do you see those stars? That is him telling you how strong he is. Can you feel my heart? That is him telling you about his love.

His arm, dearest one, has not grown shorter, nor has his strength grown less! He has not forgotten us, for he has sent us his only Son and given him over as a prey to death.

Let us swear to put our faith in him, always. Let us swear never to allow the rock of hope to crumble away within us. Even when everything seems impossible. Even when he hides to increase our loving thirst. Even when sorrow batters at the gate. Always.

Come, let us kneel on this tree-trunk beside the spring and repeat the words which we shall keep repeating to him throughout our lives:

Lord, I know you love me!
Lord, you know I love you!

* * *

And now I want us to make a promise together. An absolute, all-embracing, binding promise, to be renewed on our wedding-night. Here it is:

'Lord, we shall think of you and you will think of us.'

We shall think of your glory, of the spreading of your kingdom, of your righteousness; and you will think of our needs, of our necessities, of our tomorrow.

We forbid ourselves to worry about our own affairs but entrust them all to him. Instead, we shall worry about his righteousness and his glory, and he will give us all the rest.

Do you agree?

I made this pact when I first became aware of God's love. I can testify to you that he has never failed me and that I have lacked for nothing. Let us do it now, together.

And Heaven will smile on our childlike faith.

12. The Uncompleted Mass

There is one truth which sums up all truths, one light which illuminates all lights, and that is:
God is love.

God is love and has, as object of his love, himself since infinitely lovable. If he had another object for his love, this would indicate the existence of a higher being than himself, which cannot be since he himself is God most Beautiful, most Great, most Holy.

Thus God loves himself as most suitably worthy of love.

God loves himself and creates the universe to the glory of his Name.

Thus we can rightly say that all creatures have been made to glorify God.

The most sublime and absolute way of glorifying God is to celebrate Mass, which is to say, to respond to the unavoidable demands of love: offering ourselves to God, sacrificing ourselves to God, communicating with God.

This is the way chosen by God himself to glorify his Name.

Hence creatures offer themselves, sacrifice them-

selves and communicate to glorify God; and thus
they celebrate their Mass, for this consists essen-
tially of offertory, consecration and communion.

Seen in this light, the universe is nothing but a
huge altar on which occurs a countless series of
sacrifices, running throughout the history of all na-
tions – a history which can be summed up like this:

> God loves the creature and creates him,
> the creature loves his God and gives himself.
> God loves the creature and redeems him,
> the creature loves his God and sacrifices himself.
> God loves the creature and unites with him,
> the creature loves his God and accepts the union.

Celebrating a true Mass, therefore, means offering
ourselves, sacrificing ourselves and communicating
for love of God.

This is the meaning of all life in the light of God's
loving will.

*   *   *

The creature's sacrifice (his Mass) has had four
distinct historic stages:

a) before Adam sinned;

b) after he sinned and before the coming of
Christ;

c) during Christ's life on earth;

d) after Christ's departure.

Before the advent of sin.

The sacrifice was one of praise and adoration. At the virginal dawn of the world, this was the law that the creatures breathed. Self-offering, self-sacrifice and communion were spontaneous. Before the majesty of God, the creature felt himself to be a debtor and adoration was his fundamental attitude. So strong was the conviction that God alone exists that praise was mingled with the desire to be self-effacing and to disappear. Such was the fundamental humility of creatures.

The inanimate creation celebrated its own Mass unawares, by obeying the law of nature, which is the law of God and which in itself comprehends adoration of God as a basic constituent element.

The flower that fades, the plant that dies, the animal that gives its flesh to nourish a different kind of animal, are acts of adoration offered to the Divine Lawgiver, who has ordered all things in wonderful wisdom and immeasurable power. In the silence of my adoring soul, I seem to hear an echo of the joy imbuing all inanimate creatures at the moment when they fulfilled the ends to which they were created. Might not the grass in its mute language have said to the sheep browsing on it: Take me, I gladly give myself since my end is to be inside you?

And man? As nature's conscious priest, he was aware of the great drama of adoration and praise surrounding him and lovingly inviting him to celebrate his own sacrifice.

What joy in offering himself to the majestic progress of his God! What bliss in the desire to sacrifice, to annihilate himself out of love for him who alone is, who alone can, who alone knows!

The life of man and things was the first uncompleted Mass, celebrated in the Eden of the world, 'while the morning stars in chorus sang their praises'.

* * *

Then came sin.

Sin in the ultimate analysis is the refusal to celebrate the true Mass, that is, a refusal to adore, to praise and to plead with God.

Man, nature's priest, upset the altar of worship.

The earth became a den of thieves, of thieves who pilfered God's glory.

Man built another altar and on it placed himself, seeking to offer this idol the glory stolen from God.

The glory was false and mendacious.

But the memory of the first, joyful, peace-conferring sacrifice kept coming back with irresistable force. The need for it gnawed at his vitals, seemingly part of man's innate nature. It was irresistible.

Not knowing quite why, men began building altars out of doors and offering sacrifices to their God, who in any case was by no means dead.

All the peoples of the world built altars of this sort. Hence a traveller might say: I have seen cities without walls, cities without arts, but never a people without sacrifices.

It was a need allowing of no respite.

Man raised altars, summoned his family, tribe,

nation round them and, having become a priest (that is to say, mankind's representative before God), on them offered lambs, goats, baskets of first-fruits, plates of best-quality flour or vases of honey extracted from the comb.

His confidence shaken by the reality of sin, he raised his hands to heaven and said: 'O almighty and eternal God, I believe in you, I love you. Accept these gifts in the name of my people, accept . . .'

But this was not enough.

Sin's shadow fell immediately back over man. The shadow tormented him since it seemed to him as if his God had withdrawn from him.

What shall I do? Is there anything in the world which can cancel sin? O that the water of all the seas, lakes and streams would suffice! Perhaps if I used hyssop or lye . . . No, still not enough.

And if I use fire, can fire burn sin away?

The answer is always the same: No, no, no.

And if I use blood? That is the most precious of liquids, the very symbol of life . . .

And he used blood.

On his altars, atoning victims were substituted for peaceful ones and the knives of the priests never rested from opening the throats and veins of harmless, gentle beasts.

A bloody river flooded the world, nor was there departure or disaster, or harvest or thanksgiving that did not have an accompanying sacrifice, that is to say, an offering, a slaughtering, a consuming of victims.

*　　*　　*

A river of blood . . .

Yet all that blood did not remotely redden the ocean of God.

It was but a symbol of congenital helplessness, and its only justification lay in the intentions of man who offered it.

A different sort of blood was needed.

The lambs slaughtered over the thousands of years since Adam had risen to astronomical figures but . . . one Lamb was lacking.

The true Lamb . . .

Mankind realised that their sacrifices were merely symbolic, symbolic of a sacrifice yet to come, which would consummate them all, give value to them all and raise them to true worship.

And in the fulness of time . . . came Christ.

Christ 'like a hero to run his race', like the sun rising in the darkness, like water falling on dry ground, came into the world like a new world.

He was God and he was man. He was the Son of God and Son of Man.

As God he had the power to annihilate sin, as man the right to stand in surety for all his scapegrace brothers.

He burnt up the stages of his life with one sole fire devouring him, the desire 'to do the Father's will', that is to say, to celebrate his Mass, and in haste ascended the altar of the world: Calvary.

He took two pieces of wood and made a pair of scales.

Then he dragged this up to the hill, he alone knowing what had to be done.

On Calvary he offered his hands as the scale-
pans. In one he put all the sins of mankind and in
the other all his Blood.

'Is the balance correct?' he asked the Father.

And the voice of the ages replied:

'Beata cuius brachiis
pretium perpendit saeculi
statera facta corporis
tulitque praedam tartari.'

And Tartarus gave up its prey.

Jesus, the new Adam, had celebrated his Mass,
the true Mass. Masses celebrated before him had
only been symbolic of his; those celebrated after him
were to be the renewal of his.

God turned his face to smile on mankind.

*   *   *

And since then?

Since then it has been our Mass, since Jesus's
Mass is incomplete.

Yes, incomplete, for as St. Paul says, 'In my own
flesh I supplement what is lacking to the sufferings
of Christ!'

Is there then still something missing in that infinite offering, consecration and consummation performed by Jesus?

Yes, mine, yours, our future family's is missing.

You see, Christ's sacrifice is like a limitless ocean.
It is infinite since the Victim's value is infinite, but

to this sacrifice God's love wills to unite the little, infinitely little sacrifice of man, Christ's brother. To
the sacrifice of the Head, he wills to unite the
sacrifice of the Members of the Mystical Body. This
is like adding one drop to the infinite sea. It is very
small, a mere nothing, but right that this should be
thus, since he has willed that it should be so.

And besides, this helps to make us courageous
and to give a meaning to our sorrows. For these on
their own would be dispersed in time into
nothingness, but united to Christ remain forever to
sing the glory of God.

For you know, everything is to his glory.

When each evening we gather up our scraps of
suffering as we gather up scraps of bread when food
is scarce, and store them away for the dawn of the
following day, I think we give glory to God.

And when the priest makes his offering and we
give him these crumbs to add to his, we shall be
glorifying God.

And when the priest, becoming Christ present in
history, transforms that bread into his Body by the
all-powerful words of consecration, our sufferings
fused with Christ's sufferings will glorify God.

And so on, until the end of the world, until the
sacrifice of the last predestined individual, until the
'perfect stature' of the Mystical Body has been
achieved.

13.   The Psalmody of Patience

We set out before sunrise. The air was cold and still.

Damp and gleaming with the dews of night, the track led us up to the pastures in less than half an hour. We didn't meet a living soul. The shepherds were still asleep. Only the acrid smell of sheep in the air.

Silently we crossed their terrain, taking a path across the meadows.

Dawn began to break in the eastern sky, a dawn as delicate as the lace in the cradle waiting for a newborn child.

You strode along beside me with all the energy of youth, keeping pace with me, though I was more used to walking in the mountains.

We said our prayers, reciting the eighth Psalm:

'Yahweh our Lord,
    how glorious your name throughout the world!
Compared with the skies created by your fingers
    and the moon and stars fixed by you in space,
what is man, for you to spare a thought for him,
    a human being, for you to care for him?'

By now the sun had risen and the path lay ahead, easy and cheerful. We had breakfast beside a stream and went on straight away.

The rucksack began to make its weight felt; the heat could be felt too. The grass became sparser with the naked rock appearing here and there.

Round a corner – the stone quarry.

We cross this, jumping from stone to stone, trying not to lose our balance and finish up with quite a few scratches on our legs.

After the quarry, we enter a difficult gully with rocky sides.

Progress becomes slower and the gradient extremely sharp.

The sun beats down on our shoulders and makes us sweat.

The further we go, the hotter, more hostile, unstable and treacherous the ground becomes.

We climb on in silence. Turning round, I see a lock of your hair plastered across one cheek with sweat. I ask if you would like to stop but you reply that you would rather go on. It seems to me at that moment that I can feel your tiredness in my legs.

The gully becomes steeper and steeper and the heat more suffocating. The flinty ground, a mixture of fallen rocks and rubbish brought down by the stream, offers no firm foothold to our hobnailed boots and makes it even harder work than ever. I ask for your rucksack, so that I can carry both, but you won't agree: you want to share the fatigue equally.

We go on for another hour, not saying much to conserve our energy.

You were sweating so much, it was running down your lovely face, while your eyes, slightly inflamed by the glare from the rocks, looked burning and determined.

We roped ourselves together for the last part of the gully.

When I tied the climbing rope round your waist, I could tell from your heavy breathing that you were straining every muscle.

The rock gave us respite somewhat but increased the glare of the sunlight.

Slowly, slowly, from fingerhold to fingerhold we climbed.

I felt as if I had something sacred tied to my rope and found the thought intoxicating.

What a fine thing it is to be climbing together, I exclaimed after a difficult spell.

You were really wonderful, struggling up! I could see your hands grasping for each crevice as your muscles strained under the white skin. When you couldn't manage and I tried to help you with the rope, you gave me such a grateful look.

The horizon by now was enormous and a wonderful view appeared before our eyes once we reached the crest of the gully and could see over the sides.

We attacked the rock-wall on the left as our final task of the day.

Here we went more carefully as it was more dangerous.

We reached a vertical part where we had to put crampons in the rock to keep going.

You were marvellous: in spite of being tired, you

lithely tackled the vertical rock face, taking advantage of the minutest features.

The last part of the climb tried our strength to the utmost. Crevices, toeholds, glare, heat, sweat, abrasions, strain, up, up, with clenched teeth and wills harnessed to our hands, feet, knees, elbows and whole body. Our hands were bleeding where the rocks had cut them, and your face was a veritable mask of earth and sweat.

But you were more beautiful than ever, taut with the effort of our struggle, your breast heaving with the breath of youth.

As God willed, we reached the last crest, a long, almost flat crest leading to the summit, where there was still a covering of snow.

We walked along it, our feet hardly strong enough to support us, while we rubbed the snow over our hands and faces.

On the summit was a small cairn of stones.

Stretched out on the ground in the sunshine, we began to recover our strength.

We stood up: what a view!

The peaks stood like motionless giants in the sunlight. The glaciers glittered in all their splendour and the distant valleys looked like enchanted kingdoms of the human imagination.

Only prayer could express our delight and we gave vent to it with the Blessed Virgin's song:

Magnificat anima mea Dominum!

*   *   *

And on that very peak we talked about the psalmody of patience.

You began by saying, 'It's odd how the harshness of the struggle contains a treasure of joy hidden within it and coming as an unforeseen reward. The peak conquered by our muscles and brain gives us a satisfaction that we should never have known, had we made the ascent by funicular.'

The issues were good and clear and particularly pertinent to people preparing for the hard, very hard life of matrimony. We tackled them there under the Alpine sun.

To broach the matter and keep our feet firmly on the ground, I took out a letter written me by a very old friend who takes marriage seriously as a school of holiness and has in fact been married for some time. His name is Athos Carrara. And we read the letter together since it was very apposite to our discussion on patience. This is what it said:

'I work as hard as I can because there are six of us to feed, and having said this I don't think I need go into further details. My children's ages run from twelve to four, so they are at the stage when they need to be looked after like puppies, given the instinctive satisfaction they get from playing exactly like puppies; so, having worked myself into the ground, I don't let myself fall asleep on the sofa as some American fathers do. I feel it my duty to play with them, and they are never tired.

'They are completely remorseless, since not yet understanding other people's needs and I don't want to disappoint them. Sometimes I see my wife looking ashen with fatigue, but she smiles all the same and helps me play with them, and also helps with their complicated homework and with their prayers – after, it goes without saying, having done the washing up and set our cosy kitchen to rights. This happens, as you realise, after supper every day, but very often happens after lunch as well.

'Apart from all this, I have my social duties, which I must admit are very tiresome, but this can't be helped. If you love your family, you have to build your defences well beyond your own front-door. You have to be concerned about people who are already concerned about you, economically and politically for instance; and be on the alert to defend your own interests and organise your defences properly.

'And what about prayer? To this I am committed, and this is where the tension arises as far as my family is concerned. Many people complain about being tied to their family and so not being able to go out and have a good time. I don't say that I don't complain, but when I do so it's because the family prevents me from giving myself freely to serving God.

'In the morning I nearly always manage to make a good start to the day with Mass, Communion and Meditation, but never for as long as I could wish. During the day I get virtually no time for prayer until I pay a hurried visit to the Blessed Sacrament in the evening. Finally, we say the Rosary at home, with interruptions and fresh starts, depending on the moods of the children.

'My duties with the Association, visiting the poor,

almsgiving, speaking at meetings — I get through it all but breathlessly, stintedly and always with a sense of regret that I can't do it better.

'But the children, the children are the ones who have to get most used to patience and suffering.

'Children are the poorest of the poorest in the world. They are born naked, as you know, and fasting. They are born without a bean and without knowing, unable to pronounce — let alone read — a single letter. They need everything, even though they do of their own accord know when it is time to be hungry and when to go to sleep, having a single way of expressing all these needs — I mean by crying. They start life crying and, one way or another, keep right on crying. All they do is ask, complain, demand, morning, noon and night, summer and winter, from when they are a day old to when they are twenty, and a great deal longer than that. It seems as though this were the purpose for which they were born in the first place: to make their parents atone for having summoned them into existence without having asked their permission or at least their pardon.

'They are the most exacting and least grateful of the poor. Look at them playing quietly now, but you can depend on this: storms will burst suddenly. And then you have to run and arbitrate between them. Usually I try to smooth things over by saying that there is right on both sides, but this system doesn't always work.

'Look at them there so quiet, these implacable tyrants, apparently as obedient as you please, yet holding us enslaved as long as we go on drawing breath, at least as regards loving them.

'Look at those highwaymen there, each with his own temperament and his own requirements. To bring him up in the best way – which is tiring but free of anxiety – is to bring him up to love God. And this isn't easy. Each child is a world, each child a mystery.

'So, might it have been better if they had never arrived? Thank God, such a thought has never entered my head or my wife's . . .' &c.

*   *   *

I think this is enough to show the young that marriage is a serious matter and that anyone who goes into it under the impression that it will prove a fountain of delights will have another thing coming!

But let us consider this matter of trials, of struggles so liberally scattered in our lives. Why? Why suffering, diseases, poverty, the continual, sometimes even truceless strife? A whole book would of course not be enough to give an answer and for many people the answer would never come. You, however, who have lived and are living in the spirit of Christianity, will not find it hard to grasp the major aspects of this basic question.

A trial is like the climb we have just completed, tempering us, training us, getting the best out of us, making us wiser, perfecting us, making us worthy of reward, making us more like our exemplar, Jesus.

For me, my own life is evidence of this.

Listen.

When my father joined the army, my mother was left at home with four children. Life became pretty hard. We began having to do without all sorts of things and my mother had to fend for herself and us. We had to economise on everything, including new clothes. I remember, I used to wear a coarse cloth jacket of uncouth, rustic cut, with a pair of clogs on my feet, to attend intermediate school.

How shaming! I think there could hardly have been a better lesson for my vanity.

I remember, my schoolfriends always had pockets stuffed with sweets, toys, foreign stamps: not I. I could not waste time, I could not spend, I could not pause. Roped together, my brothers and sisters and I climbed straight ahead, concentrating on the essentials, following my mother's example, for she, good woman, turned her hands to every imaginable task and her mind to every ingenious makeshift.

I remember how, at the age of twelve, at the beginning of the summer holidays, without anyone's having suggested it, I got myself a job at a sawmill as a tea-boy. In three months I had earned the price of my books for the following year and firewood for the whole winter.

When I think back on those times, I am convinced that they were most valuable ones for me and for my family, since they laid solid foundations for us to build on.

Have you ever wondered why God, who is so loving, so generous and so powerful, allows families to

experience so many trials in this world? Why nine-
tenths of mankind have to struggle so hard for the
necessities of life?

Apart from sinful poverty, known as misery,
nearly always due to vice or to social injustice, why
so many people spend their whole life absorbed in
the daily struggle for enough to eat?

I think this shows a loving providence.

If we were comfortable and rich, it would be hard
for us to abide by the law of God; it would be hard
for us to obtain the results which with so much
hardship we do obtain.

Think how hard it is to train a rich boy!

To be frank, I have never wished wealth on any
boy! There is no worse an environment for anyone
young than comfort.

Look at the Church: her best children are
recruited from the poor, from those who are used to
making sacrifices. If you were to study the lives of
her bishops, you would have very evident proof of
what is meant by 'the school of heroism'.

Besides, if Jesus says, 'Woe to the rich!' who are
you and I to contradict him?

I think the ideal conditions for building a family
are dignified poverty, just that: at the mean-point
between misery and wealth.

And no one can take this away from us if we are
faithful to God.

Misery is almost always an affliction and to avoid
this we only have to be united with God and put our
trust in him. God doesn't promise us a comfortable
life; he assures us of our food, that is to say, of the

necessities for fulfilling our vocation – and that is enough.

Let us therefore stay serene, in the thought that we are in a powerful hand, and go forward joyfully to live our lives.

14.   Mary, the True Church

Accursed was the womb of Eve.

Blessed, the womb of Mary.

The first at the dawn of creation, the second at the dawn of redemption.

The former, contorted in giving birth to Cain, the latter joyfully exultant in giving birth to Jesus. The former was full of earth, the latter full of heaven. Eve's womb had sucked in a deadly fruit, Mary's womb breathed in the Living Spirit.

*   *   *

One day, at the beginning of the world, God drew woman out of man to be the mother of his children.

Earth became a kingdom with a king and queen. Everything belonged to them.

But there was a law in that kingdom, a law established by the Giver of all things. The law was called 'order'. Man could own things, but in the established order, for an established end.

He could own food, to keep him alive. The pleasure of having food was to be a product, not the end.

He could own woman, for the procreation of life. The pleasure of owning woman was to be the product, not the end.

In a word, pleasure was to be a means, not the end, a product, not the principle. It was to be like a drop of oil, giving more flexibility to human action, not something sought in itself.

In other words, this meant: first God, then man; first His will, then man's will; first loving God, then loving human beings.

Exactly as Jesus was later to put it: 'First seek the kingdom of God and his righteousness, and everything else will be added to you later.'

But then came temptation and the form it took was the temptation to rebel.

Man put himself in God's place and upset the order of things.

Disorder was born.

Sin is disorder: precisely that.

Man no longer ate to live, he lived to eat.

He didn't drink to live, he lived to drink.

But where this disorder was worst of all was in his ownership of the creature nearest to him: woman, his queen.

Looking at woman, he no longer sought the children of his love which should have been born of her, but the pleasure inherent in the sexual act.

Placing pleasure before the Law, he upset the order of things.

In the place of God's legislation, he put man's legislation.

What a terrible thing to do!

The world became a menagerie of wild beasts, greedy for unrestrained pleasure; war supplanted peace; life gave way to death.

And thus man was condemned to die.

Yet the desire for that peace, the yearning for that life, lingered on.

And that desire and yearning took on a face: a woman's face.

'A woman will come and she will bear a son,' was God's revelation to console mankind in its exile, 'and this child will be the saviour of his people.'

If only that woman would come, the generations were to repeat, tormented by evil and helpless to extricate themselves.

A thousand years went by . . . Nothing happened.

Mankind's arms raised in supplication were like lightning conductors waiting for the divine spark.

Two thousand years went by . . . Nothing happened!

When will she come? Where will she appear? Why, O Heavens, remain sealed? Why deaf to the pleadings of mankind? Yes, we have sinned, but you should hear us. As the east is distant from the west, so is the scope of your compassion.

Three thousand years went by . . . Nothing happened!

O Heavens, rain down the Righteous One! O Earth, split open and bring forth the Saviour!

O almighty and eternal God, hear the prayers of your people. How much longer will you be angry with us? How much longer will your wrath ravage our tents? O, give us a sign! For love of your Anointed, give us a sign!

Do you want a sign, asks the prophet Isaiah. Here it is: 'A virgin will bear a son.'

The face of all men's hopes, the heart of all his loves, the purity of all purity, the beauty of all beauties, were acquiring a heart, a face, a purity, a beauty . . . Is this the awaited one?

No, that was not enough, since all matter furnished by mankind was polluted. There was no healthy spot. The world was one vast, putrid swamp.

How can you expect purity from an impure stream, or innocence from sin?

God, God alone could fashion the face, heart, purity, beauty of the creature awaited.

Four thousand years went by . . .

And God made the new creature, and it was Mary!

In Anne's womb he cut off that putrid current, running back from torrent to torrent to our first mother, Eve.

And in Anne's womb God used his almighty power to make a new creature which anew would have the virginal freshness of the original creation.

This was the Immaculate, Mary by name!

When Mary was born, it was like the birth of a new race: the race of order.

She re-established order.

Eve had enthroned mankind in place of God, Mary restored God to the throne of God.

Eve had lived to eat, Mary ate to live.

Eve had sought pleasure before sons, Mary sought the Son and set no store by pleasure, and thus she drank the poison of the Cross.

Eve had sought a leafy tree under which to sin.

Mary sought a denuded tree under which to be saved.

Eve had sought fruit fair to see but poisonous in substance.

Mary sought the unique fruit of the Cross, Christ, woeful to the eye, but sweet, how sweet!

* * *

A poor shed, with a shriek, had seen the birth of Cain, while outside rustled the accursed Serpent.

A poor shed, with a song, had seen the birth of Jesus, while outside flocked the Angels of the Lord.

* * *

Order was restored.

Mary is that re-established order.

God had made the earth as a church and Eve had reduced it to a den.

Mary was born in that den and turned it back into a church.

She herself became a church and her '*Fiat*' was the faithful echo of God's eternal '*Fiat*'.

Mary generated that new peace and was so full of love that she wanted to give that sweet and precious peace to others.

A price was set on this: the Son.

Mary consented and offered her Son.

Calvary consumed the sacrifice which her love had already given.

All men would now be able to be a church, that is to say, become Temples of God.

All they had to do was accept the Law of Order: God first, then man; first life and the multiplication of life, then pleasure in life and in the multiplication of life.

Who are the married couples who accept the Law of Order? – Those who consent to have children and subordinate their pleasure to this.

Then their marriage is life, grace, peace, joy.

Who are the married couples who reject the Law of Order? – Those who want pleasure and therefore kill their children and, locked in their selfishness, lead a living death.

Their marriage is a tomb.

Mary, by the Son you offered, we beseech you, grant that many married couples may be churches and that in the morning and evening of their days they may sing:

'Virgo singularis
inter omnes mitis
nos culpis solutos
mites fac et castos!
Vitam praesta puram
iter para tutum
ut videntes Jesum
semper collactemur!'

15. Listen to the Voice

Now I have told you everything.

All the same, I'm not quite sure: it seems to me that all we have thought about together doesn't signify unless I make one point more.

You and I have written our book about the family as a church in miniature, we have pondered the lines on which this divine edifice should be built, and now we have to ask ourselves, 'Is this the life for us?'

Is it to be a reality or remain a dream?

Am I to feel you beside me as my future wife, or am I to think of you as the sweet image of an individual vocation to love God?

Am I to squeeze you in my arms, or know the weight of a renunciation all the greater for having known you, by taking another path, alone?

So we must put the question: Is there another way, outside marriage?

There certainly is, as well you know: the way of virginity, the way of total renunciation, the way where loving God becomes so absorbing as to take the place even of married love.

This is the mystery of the great call, in answer to

which the soul shuts itself up in the cabin of its own heart, feeling an irresistible desire to be alone with God; this is its answer to the call whispered by God within the soul, a secret summons known only to a few.

It is a strange way, willed by God in his inscrutable designs, a way followed by very few before the coming of Christ and by many ever since.

You remember what I said about the cavity dug by God near the human heart? A cavity making us feel we need that part of ourselves which is outside us and which is called wife? Well, when God wills, this cavity becomes so vast that it can be filled only by God himself, who is infinite. It is extraordinary what happens: under God's touch, man becomes caught in a vortex of love making his days fly past and flinging him into eternity, where as Jesus says, 'There will be neither wife nor husband, but they will all be angels of God.'

Unable to dispense with this most essential gamut of love embodied in married love, the soul transfers all the relationships previously experienced with creatures to God, calling God her husband and saying to him what she originally sang to the part of her which would have completed her in marriage.

'I love you' is the key-phrase of that sweetest of conversations, established between the soul and God; and between the two is woven a relationship of which marriage is the perfect image.

If you read the mystics, you will find this one phrase, faithfully echoing that greatest of love poems, I mean the *Song of Songs*.

'I loved you when you were a child
and bound you to me with eternal chains.'

Awe-inspiring the way of virginity, yet smooth,
hard yet very sweet, harsh yet beguiling.

For the soul who has responded to the divine summons, married love is no more; were she to accept it,
this would be a compromise and her sin would be
that of treachery and adultery.

Such is the way of virginity, and he who chooses it
may not turn back. Woe to him if he does! Have you
ever thought how sad it must be for religious who
are luke-warm? To have renounced both the human
and the divine, compromising both with heaven and
with earth, brides of Christ betraying his love for
another?

No, no, no! No one is obliged to choose this way,
but once you have chosen it, you cannot turn back.
It is like a marriage, binding until death. Absolute
faith becomes the law.

Who chooses the way of virginity must realise that
it is an awesome way, the way of the limitless
glaciers, the way of solitude, the way of heroism, the
way of total dismemberment, the way of sacrifice,
the way in which, day by day, we die to heart, body
and spirit.

Yet, sweetest of ways! A way where the Divine
Lover often hides, to make your thirst for love grow
all the stronger; but when he reappears, and knocks
on your door, his caresses outdo all caresses with
kisses to conquer all kisses and fruitfulness surpassing all fruitfulness.

Your room will be ablaze with love and you yourself caught up in him, melting in measureless,
timeless conversation, even though, day by day, he
treats you with renewed, almost divine severity, af-
fecting you like that echoing cry of the Scriptures:
'Do you not know that your God is a jealous God?'

If you only knew how God knows how to love!

If you only knew how domineering, how
overwhelming, how he knows how to dig down
deeper and deeper to conquer every part of you, to
burn all the dross away: all memories, all yearnings,
all the past, all selfishness, all fears, to make his
pure, purest of pure, love blaze forth alone!

A great way, but a very awesome one!

*   *   *

But which is the better one?

Which one should we follow?

The first or the second?

Ought we to build our home, our miniature
church, or should we renounce it?

It seems to me that the right answer is this: The
best way is the one which He wills for each of us; the
best way is His most sweet will.

Is marriage better, or virginity?

A truce to the endless discussions about which
way is superior to the other! To my mind, these only
feed our collective pride. To my mind, this is
transforming the life of heaven into a race between
envious competitors, who look down pityingly on
those who don't belong to their own team!

Is marriage better, or virginity? The question is misconceived, since theoretical, and doesn't help me solve my own problem.

It is more accurate to say: What does God want of me? What is his design for me?

If he wants me to get married, this is the better way for me. If he wants me to renounce marriage, that is the way for me. In a word, the better way is the Will of God.

*　　　*　　　*

This being so, we must make a fundamental point forthwith. We must not too eagerly or lightly renounce the first summons of the two, i.e. the one to marriage. We must remember that for that summons we have very plain words, amounting to a command.

Let us listen for a moment and meditate on them calmly.

Said God, 'It is not good for the man to be alone.'

And again: 'This is why a man leaves his father and mother and clings to his wife, and they become one body.'

And again, 'Be fruitful, multiply and populate the earth.'

Here God is speaking directly in very precise terms. He commands us not to stay on our own, but to marry and have children.

There are people who, without so much as discussing it, exclude marriage from their lives. Yet these quite often give themselves out for Christians. They are afraid of women, but call this 'purity'.

They are lazy and do not want the bother of a household, and call this 'renunciation'.

They are sick and do not feel the need for children, and this they call 'virginity'.

There are others who will not entertain the idea of marriage because they think of it as a way for second-rate people. These are very dangerous to the Church, since they are as proud as Satan and present themselves daily before the Lord's altar with these grand words: 'Lord, I thank you that I am not like everyone else, and especially that I am not like that poor devil down there at the back who has a wife and four children and allows himself the pleasures of the flesh.

'I have never got married because I want to keep those incarnate devils known as women at arms length, and I have regularly offered you the adoration of a soul as beautiful and candid as spring-water.'

For people like this, the Old Testament might not exist; only the New for them, and in the New they humbly and unworthily allocate themselves the place of John leaning on Jesus's bosom.

Everything is transposed and – twist, twist, scrape, scrape – at a given moment they make the discovery that the whole universe is revolving round them.

This is what St. Bernard called the eighth degree of pride. The climb to heaven, intimacy with God, sacrifice, even the Cross, even martyrdom, but not for love of God – for love of self; not for the triumph of God but the triumph of self with God.

Look, says the soul thus deluded, what is the world? – Dust.

Earthly glory? – Vapour. Wealth? – Sand. One thing alone is worthwhile, to leap, to leap up to God, to be near him, and thence to look down on all the sinners at your feet, crushed by the power of God. And thence to contemplate your own triumph, that being identical with God's.

This is the most fearful form of pride that can ever take root in a soul. To be with God, to serve God, to sacrifice ourselves for God, but not for love of him but love of us.

And certain it is that when this sort of pride gnaws at the soul, then marriage is looked down on. It is too humble a kind of life, too hidden, too unworthy. People become capable of not even seeing their own fathers and mothers in a true light . . . and thus turn into demons.

No, no, in choosing our vocation we must not allow ourselves to be influenced by vanity or pride. Let us be humble and begin by saying, 'I have so little virtue that I am not fit for the way of virginity, nor am I for that of marriage, and if God does not uphold me with his hand, how can I know what to do? How can I succeed? How can I build a Christian family?'

Then you will hear a voice saying, 'Take heart! God commands you to build a family and, if he commands, he will give you all the means for doing what he commands. You will lack nothing.' A voice will come, make no doubt of it, and prompt you to take the way which God has chosen for you.

But it may also happen that another voice will come, another call, insistent and allowing you no peace, 'No, there is another way for you. You must renounce having a family. I have made another plan for you. Listen to me.'

'But, O Lord, in Scripture you have commanded me to marry and have children! How am I to act?'

'Look, for you I have a counter-order. I have another way and I command you to take it.'

And the voice becomes so powerful and the order so insistent that no further doubt is possible and you choose this other way.

Oh, Christians need not fear, need not think that God's voice can't make itself heard. If they are single-hearted and do not make matters so complicated, everything will turn out as it should, since God is love and will not forsake us.

In the one case or the other, God's voice will be clear and distinct, provided that . . .

*   *   *

Provided that we want to do his will and not our own.

At this point I have no fear of saying that man begins to see his own affairs clearly, the day when he decides absolutely and completely to accept the meaning of the prayer taught us by Jesus.

'Father, . . . your will be done.'

When these words cease to be a mere dream and become a 'living prayer' light dawns in the soul.

It may be that this moment hasn't come yet, it

may be that the decision is still a long way off, it
may be that we are not mature enough yet to make
an enlightened choice, but the very acceptance of
waiting may itself be 'doing God's will'. Doesn't acceptance of a long period of indecision mean
trusting in God's activity as he prepares our
tomorrow from one day to the next?

Of course this isn't easy. Even the saints had
difficulties over this.

Worried over the question of his vocation, St. Ber-
nardino of Siena lost his health and peace of mind.
Later, when he had grown mature, thinking back on
those early days and on his impatience, he said, 'I
ought to have had more confidence in my Lord. I
wasn't mature enough then to understand God's
answer. If only I had been more patient!' Then,
repeating the words of Scripture, he said, 'How
sweet it is in silence to await the saving work of
God!'

And if our impatience makes the waiting less than
sweet and if the sealed heavens make our poor, weak
faith vacillate, oh, then there's one good way of
fighting to improve our positions in the spiritual
combat.

Look, there is the way of love, the way of charity.

Brother, don't worry too much about what to do.
Try loving instead. Don't keep badgering Heaven
with useless questions: Which is to be my road?
Make a point of loving instead.

By loving, you will discover which way yours is to
be, by loving you will hear the Voice, by loving you
will find peace.

Love is the fulfilment of the Law and the rule of all life, the solution to every problem, the stimulus to all holiness.

Strengthen your love, give yourself to your brother-men, seek out the poor, immerse yourself in the dough of the world like a generous leaven, come out of yourself, come out of your cave, do not seek selfish pleasure, do not think about yourself all the time, don't think of yourself as the centre of the universe.

Learn the way of self-giving.

In giving yourself, you will find God, and he and he alone will be able to tell you which your vocation is to be, so that you can achieve total self-giving in the best and most appropriate way for you.

*   *   *

Brothers, sisters . . .
Listen to the voice!